LOST PLAYS   (1913-1915)

EUGENE O'NEILL

LOST PLAYS

OF

EUGENE O'NEILL

The Citadel Press • **New York**

FIRST PAPERBOUND EDITION 1963

Library of Congress Catalog Card Number 58-8022
Manufactured in the United States of America
Published by The Citadel Press,
222 Fourth Avenue, New York 3, N. Y.

CONTENTS

PAGE

INTRODUCTION

EUGENE O'NEILL, the playwright, first came into view in 1916, at the Wharf Theatre in Provincetown, Mass. The story, often retold, is that someone had mentioned to Susan Glaspell, one of the group, that a young man had come to town with a trunkful of plays and she retorted: "We don't need a trunkful, but if he's got one good play, bring him around." "Bound East for Cardiff" was the immediate result. Other O'Neill productions quickly followed. Remaining manuscripts - the very bottom layer of the "trunkful" lay hidden away through the years. And here they are, brought to light at last, exactly as they were originally written and tossed into that magical trunk almost four decades ago.

We are not, like latecomers to a rich banquet, gathering leftovers from the table. Rather, we enjoy, from the vantage point of the plays here presented an Alice in Wonderland-like serving of the hors d'ouvres, the first course on the menu, last.

Every circumstance favored O'Neill beyond the good fortune of most writers. He had early served apprenticeship in the old theatre. He could sift and cull elements essential for his historical mission to remold the very face of our theatre in his own image.

Theodore Dreiser, earlier in the century had fought the first great round for realistic interpretation of the American scene. His "Sister Carrie" was throttled "aborning." But the indomitable warrior had bided his time and after ten years of enforced silence, was once more in the van of the struggle.

It was an impelling movement, more significant than any that preceded it, and would outlive the whole procession of literary fashions yet to come, dada-ism, futurism, impressionism, expressionism, existentialism, and all the other obscure isms, parasitic air-plant cults without roots anywhere, precious and perishable. The Dreiser school was an expression of ideals based on a collective American conscience - and since it had as its chief purpose the welfare of the many as opposed to the individualistic doctrinaires, it had a deeper foundation, powerful, stimulating and enduring.

Little magazines were mushrooming in New York, Chicago, San Francisco and elsewhere to rally behind Dreiser. The time had come for a general onslaught to liberate American letters from the all-pervading sunshine philosophy and childish evasion of grim reality. Actually the Wharf Theatre in Provincetown was a part of this movement. Young O'Neill quite naturally gravitated toward this influence while still groping for artistic perception, power and maturity. Moreover, the Provincetown group had a ready-made laboratory awaiting him, to lead along the new paths, already indicated by Dreiser, toward the objective social documentation that is one of O'Neill's most significant contributions to the modern theatre.

I would not wish it implied that in my critical judgment I consider the plays in this volume masterpieces. However, within certain limitations, in invention, power of execution, and psychological intensity, these early flights of O'Neill are truly startling.

The first play in the volume marks the emergence of the serious, "slice of life" drama in America. In technique it is the stage counterpart of the Edgar Allen Poe short story, almost a century old. O'Neill evolved it from the "vaudeville sketch" type of entertainment which flourished like Jonah's gourd-vine in the 'teen years of our century. It organizes with complete unity of time, place and purpose - everything revolving around one central theme, like rubber tightly wound around the core of a golf ball. Young O'Neill demonstrates not only his keen perception of life on different social levels, but his full realization of the relationships as well, in terms of diametrically opposed interests and their inherent basic conflicts. He is no soap box orator, yet he can fashion a sociological capsule. "Here's the nub" he seems to say, "and what are you, you, you and *you* going to do about it?" Little wonder then that an old lady upon viewing O'Neill in the theatre for the first time, exclaimed, "Who wants to hear about those terrible people he writes about! Why he succeeded in ruining my entire evening!" In "Abortion" he actually anticipates Dreiser's "American Tragedy" by a dozen years!

To the next play in the volume, little need be added here. "The Movie Man" is O'Neill early caught in a rare, playful mood - he banters and ridicules the foibles of Hollywood. And the most remarkable thing about it all is that actually O'Neill could anticipate from the shadowy embryonic form at this writing . . . 1914, the swollen monstrosity to come.

In "The Sniper" we have a full-voiced protest against War, from the little people who have ever suffered most from it. Through the eyes of a half-wit, the madness, stupidity, waste and horror are exposed - we see a kaleidoscope of devastating explosion, panic, rush for shelter, bodies of the torn victims. It all has particular significance today - perhaps it isn't yet too late for us to ponder and profit by it!

The short play form obviously could not serve the larger statement young O'Neill feels impelled to make in the fourth play of the group here. It is a full portrait study of a literary lion, who would guide others through unchartered country and paradoxically is himself in need of guidance . . . A broader canvas is needed and our playwright accepts the challenge and moves forward boldly. "Servitude" is in conventional three act form, surprisingly smooth in construction - the dialogue rich with typical, incisive O'Neill characterization. Here is an O'Neill play with a happy ending! Yet throbbing and vital beyond most items of the theatre today.

And finally, we come to the last play in the volume . . ."A Wife for a Life." In point of chronology it takes precedence over all the others here. It is written in 1913 - O'Neill's very first play! It is not so much an O'Neill work as it is a product of the "Drayma" as O'Neill finds it at the very start of his career. (*Side by side comparison of this period piece with any of the other plays presented here will indicate the extent of the debt our contemporary theatre owes to O'Neill.*) He hewed to the wood faithfully in the pattern of the then

INTRODUCTION

current vaudeville sketches. Certainly he succeeds in making it creak and groan with the best of them; the heavy-handed stage business, the stilted dialogue, the windjammer soliloquy - all as dated as high button shoes. Yet there's one distinguishing feature. The O'Neill opus has no villain! To a generation long sermonized that villainy must inevitably be punished, young O'Neill's substitution of a time and circumstance philosophy is unacceptable. Little wonder then that the vaudeville magnates ignore the opus, and it falls still-born from the budding play-smith's pen. O'Neill turns his back on commercial theatre for-ever! It is the critical juncture in his career, perhaps the most significant move in our theatre annals as well.

Finally, the uncovering of this important group of O'Neill "firsts" is an outstanding publishing event. Aside from adding to the rich store of our theatre repertoire, this volume furnishes invaluable material for understanding and evaluating the "grow-ing pains" period of O'Neill in relation to the development of our entire field of native Drama.

LAWRENCE GELLERT

"ABORTION" (1914)

A Play In One Act

Characters

JACK TOWNSEND

JOHN TOWNSEND, *his father.*

MRS. TOWNSEND, *his mother.*

LUCY TOWNSEND, *his sister.*

EVELYN SANDS, *his fiancee.*

DONALD (BULL) HERRON, *his room-mate.*

JOE MURRAY, *a machinist.*

Students of the University.

Evelyn Sands, Jack girl

The action takes place in the study of the suite of rooms occupied by Townsend and Herron on the ground floor of a dormitory in a large eastern university in the United States.

Time - The Present.

11

SCENE: *The study of the suite of rooms occupied by Jack Townsend and Donald Herron on the ground floor of a dormitory in a large eastern university of the United States. The left wall is composed almost entirely of a large bow-window looking out on the campus, and forming a window seat which is piled high with bright colored cushions. In the middle of the far side, a door opening into a hallway of the dormitory. On either side of the door, leather covered divans with leather cushions. In the right corner to the rear, a writing desk with an electric drop-light hanging over it. In the middle of the right wall, a fireplace. In the extreme right foreground, a door opening into a bedroom. In the center of the room, a table with an electric reading-lamp wired from the chandelier above. Books, periodicals, pipes, cigarette boxes, ash-trays, etc., are also on the table. The walls of the room are hung with flags, class banners, framed photographs of baseball and football teams, college posters, etc. Two Morris chairs and several rockers are grouped about the table.*

It is about eight o'clock in the evening of a warm day in June. At first the windows on the left are gray with the dim glow of the dying twilight but as the action progresses this slowly disappears.

A sound of voices comes from the hall. The door in the rear is opened and Mrs. Townsend and Lucy enter, escorted by Herron. Their figures can be vaguely made out in the dusk of the room.

LUCY. (*Feeling her way toward the table*) "Do put on the lights, Bull! I know I'm going to break my neck in a minute." (*Mrs. Townsend remains standing by the doorway.*)

HERRON. (*Cheerfully*) "One minute, one minute!" (*Strikes his shin against the corner of the divan - wrathfully*) "Oh - " (*Bites his tongue just in time.*)

LUCY. *(With a gurgling laugh)* "Say it! Say it!"

HERRON. *(Leaning over the divan and feeling on the wall for the electric switch - softly)* "Oh darn!"

LUCY. "Hypocrite! That isn't what you were going to say."

HERRON. "Oh gosh, then." *(Finds the switch)* "There!" *(Turns on all the lights except the drop-light)* "Let there be light!"

LUCY. *(She is a small, vivacious blond nineteen years old, gushing with enthusiasm over everything and everybody. She wears an immense bouquet of flowers at the waist of her dark blue dress and carries a flag)* "Don't stand there posing, Bull." *(Flings herself into one of the Morris chairs)* "You look much more like a God of darkness than one of light."

MRS. TOWNSEND. *(A sweet-faced, soft-spoken, gray-haired lady in her early fifties. She is dressed in dark gray. She turns to Lucy with smiling remonstrance)* "Lucy!" *(To Herron who clumsily arranges a cushion at the back of a rocking chair for her)* "Thank you, Donald." *(Herron winces at the "Donald.")*

LUCY. *(Contemptuously)* "Donald!"

HERRON. *(Chuckling - He is a huge, swarthy six-footer with a bull neck and an omnipresent grin, slow to anger and to understanding but - an All-American tackle. His immense frame is decked out in white flannels which make him look gigantic.)* "I don't care much for the 'Donald' myself."

LUCY. "And I still claim, Mother, that Donald, alias Bull, resembles Pluto more than any other divinity. It is true, judging from the pictures I have seen, that Pluto was not as fat -" *(As Herron slouches into a sitting position on the divan)* "nor as clumsy, but -"

HERRON. *(Grinning)* "What have I done today? What have I done? Didn't I purchase candy and beautiful flowers? And now I reap nothing but abuse. I appeal to you, Mrs. Townsend. She is breaking me on the wheel."

LUCY. "Poor butterfly!" *(Convulsed with laughter)* "Ha ha ha! Poor, delicate fragile butterfly!"

HERRON. "There you go again!" *(Appealingly)* "You see, Mrs. Townsend? Every word of mine is turned to mockery." *(He sighs explosively.)*

MRS. TOWNSEND. *(Smiling)* "Never mind, Donald; you ought to hear the nice things she says behind your back."

LUCY. *(Indignantly)* "Mother!"

HERRON. "I find it hard to believe."

LUCY. "Mother is fibbing so as not to hurt your feelings." *(with a roguish smile)* "I never, never in all my life said a good word about you. You don't deserve it."

MRS. TOWNSEND. "Why, Lucy, what a thing to say!" *(While she is speaking Joe Murray appears in the doorway to the rear. He is a slight, stoop-shouldered, narrow-chested young fellow of eighteen, with large, feverish, black eyes, thin lips, pasty complexion, and the sunken cheeks of a tuberculosis victim. He wears a shabby dark suit. He peers blinkingly around the room and knocks but they do not hear him.)*

LUCY. *(Glancing toward the door and seeing him)* "Someone to see you, Bull."

HERRON. *(Turning to Murray)* "Anything you want?"

MURRAY. *(Aggresively)* "I wanta see Townsend, Jack Townsend."

HERRON. "He's not here."

MURRAY. "D'yuh know when he'll be in?"

HERRON. "Any minute; but I advise you not to wait. He

won't have any time for you tonight. If you want to leave a message I'll give it to him."

MURRAY. (*Truculently*) "He'll find time for me all right."

HERRON. (*Staring at him*) "You think so? Suit yourself." (*Pointedly*) "You can wait for him *outside*." (*Murray's face pales with rage. He starts to say something then turns abruptly and disappears into the hallway.*)

HERRON. "Pleasant little man!"

LUCY. "Don't you know who it was?"

HERRON. "Never saw him before; probably some fresh 'townie' who thinks Jack's indebted to him because he recovered a stolen baseball bat or something, and wants to put the acid on him for a dollar or two. Jack's such a good-natured slob -"

LUCY. (*With a giggle*) "Listen to who is talking."

MRS. TOWNSEND. (*Proudly*) "Jack always has been so good-hearted."

HERRON. (*With a smile*) "He's only stingy with base-hits. Great game he pitched today. Star players usually fall down when they're captains of teams and it's their last year in college; but not old Jack - only three hits off him."

MRS. TOWNSEND. "This game we saw today decides the championship, doesn't it?"

LUCY. "Certainly, Mother. You don't suppose I'd have yelled my whole voice away if it wasn't, do you? I can hardly speak."

MRS. TOWNSEND. (*With a sly wink at Herron*) "I hadn't noticed that, Lucy." (*Herron shakes with suppressed mirth*)

LUCY. (*Pouting*) "Oh, Mother, how unkind!"

MRS. TOWNSEND. "I must confess I'm not much of a fan - Is that what you call it? - I do not understand the game and if it wasn't for Jack playing I'm afraid I would find it rather wearisome."

HERRON. "Jack is the big man of the college tonight, all right. The President is a mere nonentity beside him. Add to our list of athletic heroes one Jack Townsend, captain and pitcher."

MRS. TOWNSEND. "How they carried him around the field after the game!"

LUCY. "And cheered him!"

HERRON. "You bet we did. I had a hold of one leg. But I agree with you Mrs. Townsend. If Jack didn't play I wouldn't take much interest in baseball myself." *(Enthusiastically)* "Football is the real game."

LUCY. "Of course you'd say that."

MRS. TOWNSEND. "That's beyond me, too. I've heard it's so rough, that so many players are injured. When John first entered college his father and I made him promise not to go in for it on any account."

HERRON. *(Regretfully)* "You spoiled a fine player." *(Noise of voices from the hall)* "Speaking of the - hm - angel" *(Evelyn Sands enters followed by Jack Townsend. Evelyn is a tall, dark-haired, beautiful girl about twenty years old. Her eyes are large and brown; her mouth full-lipped, resolute; her figure lithe and graceful. She is dressed simply but stylishly in white. Jack is a well-built handsome young fellow about twenty-two years old, with blond hair brushed straight back from his forehead, intelligent blue eyes, a good-natured, self-indulgent mouth, and ruddy, tanned complexion. He has the easy confident air of one who has, through his prowess in athletics, become a figure of note in college circles and is accustomed to the deference of those around him. He wears a dark coat, white soft shirt with a bright colored tie, flannel trousers, and white tennis shoes.)*

LUCY. "Hail to the hero!" *(Evelyn comes over and sits on*

the arm of Lucy's chair. Jack stands beside his mother.)

MRS. TOWNSEND. *(Smiling fondly up at him)* "Where is your father?"

JACK. "Right outside, talking to Professor Simmons. After dinner as we were following you out of the Inn we ran into the Prof and he walked down with us. Did you think we were lost?"

LUCY. *(With a mischievous glance at Evelyn)* "We thought you might have forestalled the forthcoming happy event by eloping." *(Evelyn blushes)*

JACK. *(Laughing)* "With father for chaperon?"

LUCY. "Well, don't you dare do it! I'd never forgive you spoiling my chance to wear my gown. I'm going to be just the most stunning bridesmaid. Am I not, Mother?"

MRS. TOWNSEND. "Of course, dear." *(To Jack)* "Why didn't you ask the professor to come in?"

JACK. "I did, Mother, but he's on his way somewhere or other."

HERRON. "By the way, Jack, there was a 'townie' in here asking to see you a few minutes ago."

JACK. *(Starting nervously)* "A 'townie'? Did he give any name?"

HERRON. "No. A fresh little shrimp; said he'd wait. Wasn't he outside?"

JACK. *(Visibly uneasy)* "I didn't see anyone."

HERRON. "He'll be back probably; and look out for a touch." *(The singing of a distant quartet sounds faintly from the campus.)*

LUCY. *(Springing up)* "I hear them singing on the campus. I'm going out. Bull, when does the big P'rade start?"

HERRON. "Pretty soon; you can hear the clans gathering now."

LUCY. "I'm going to march beside them all the way to the lake."

MRS. TOWNSEND. "The lake?"

LUCY. "There's going to be a canoe carnival, and bonfires, and dancing, and everything, Mother. You've simply got to come, all of you, in honor of hero Jack."

JACK. *(Embarrassed)* "Come, come, Sis, praise from you is rare indeed."

HERRON. *(Emphatically)* "Indeed!"

LUCY. *(Archly to Herron)* "Indeed?"

MRS. TOWNSEND. *(Getting quickly from her chair - with a girlish laugh)* "I'm going with you. I'll show you young people I can celebrate with the best of you."

JACK. "Are you sure it isn't too much for you, Mother?"

MRS. TOWNSEND. *(Her face flushed with excitement)* "Non-sense, Jack!"

JACK. *(Putting his arm around her affectionately)* "Dear old mother - young mother, I should say."

LUCY. "Come on everybody!"

JACK. "You people go on ahead and I'll catch up with you." *(Mrs. Townsend goes out.)*

LUCY. *(To Herron)* "Come on, Jumbo."

HERRON. *(Groaning.)* "Jumbo! And Bull! Lucy thinks I'm a menagerie." *(He and Lucy go out. Evelyn starts to follow them but Jack stops her and takes her in his arms.)*

JACK. "We won't be alone again for ages." *(Kisses her.)*

EVELYN. *(Smiling up into his face)* "I'm so proud of you, Jack, dear."

JACK. (*Laughingly puts his fingers across her lips*) "Ssshhh! You'll give me an awful attack of exaggerated ego if you go on talking like that."

EVELYN. "But it's true, dear."

JACK. "Then for the good of my soul don't tell me. Praise from Sis is wonder enough for one day."

EVELYN. (*Moving a few steps away from him*) "I wish I could tell you how proud I felt when I sat in the grandstand and watched you." (*With a laugh*) "It was a horrid sort of selfish pride, too, for I couldn't help saying to myself from time to time: He loves me, *me*! He belongs to *me*; and I thought of how jealous all the girls around me who were singing his praises would be if they knew."

JACK. (*His face suddenly grown serious, as if at some painful memory*) "Please Evelyn! You make me feel so mean - and contemptible when you talk like that."

EVELYN. (*Astonished*) "Mean? Contemptible? How foolish you are, Jack." (*Excitedly*) "I felt like standing on my seat and shouting to all of them: 'What right have you to think of him? He is *mine, mine!*'" (*Laughing at her own enthusiasm, adds in a matter-of-fact tone*) "Or will be in three months."

JACK. (*His voice thrilling with emotion*) "In three months!" (*Jokingly*) "Do you know those three months are going to seem like three years?"

EVELYN. (*Gaily*) "Three centuries; but I was telling you how splendid you were this afternoon."

JACK. (*Protestingly*) "Sssshh, Evelyn!" (*Tries to put his arms around her.*)

EVELYN. (*Backing away and avoiding him*) "You were so cool, so brave. It struck me as symbolical of the way you would always play, in the game of life - fairly, squarely, strengthening those around you, refusing to weaken at critical moments, advancing others by sacrifices, fighting the good fight for the cause, the team, and always, always, whether vanquished or victor, reserving a hearty, honest cheer for the other side." *(Breaking off breathlessly)* "Oh, Jack dear, I loved you so!"

JACK. *(A strong note of pain in his voice, puts his hands over his ears, and forces a laugh)* "I won't listen any longer. I positively refuse."

EVELYN. *(Smiling)* "It's all over. I'm through. I simply had to tell you." *(She holds out both hands to him. He draws her into his arms and kisses her.)*

JACK. *(with deep feeling)* "I shall try - with all my strength - in the future, Evelyn, - to live as you have said and become worthy of you. Today was nothing. One does one's best for the sake of the game, for the love of the struggle. Our best happened to be luckier, more skillful, perhaps, than the other fellow's - that's all."

EVELYN. "It's so like you to say that. You're a dear." *(She kisses him. Jack's father, John Townsend, appears in the doorway. He is a tall, kindly old man of sixty or so with a quantity of white hair. He is erect, well-preserved, energetic, dressed immaculately but soberly. He laughs and shakes a finger at Evelyn.)*

TOWNSEND. "Caught in the act." *(Evelyn smiles and blushes)* "Evelyn, they're waiting for you outside and Lucy threatens to come in and drag you out if my persuasive powers have no effect. They want to make a start for the Steps and see the P'rade form. It's due to start shortly." *(While he is speaking he comes forward, puts his straw hat on the table, and sits down in one of the Morris chairs.)*

EVELYN. *(Eagerly)* "I wouldn't miss it for worlds." *(She goes to the door; then turns and looks at Jack irresolutely)*

"Aren't you coming with us, both of you?" *(Jack looks at his father uncertainly.)*

TOWNSEND. "We'll join you there; or, better still, - " *(To Jack)* "The P'rade passes right by here, doesn't it? They always used to in the old days."

JACK. "Yes, Dad."

TOWNSEND. "Then you go ahead with the others, Evelyn, and since Lucy tells me you're going to follow the P'rade, we'll be able to join you when you pass by." *(Explanatively)* "I've seen and taken part in so many of these affairs that their novelty has sort of worn off for me; and Jack, - if they were to discover the hero of the day at this stage of the game he wouldn't have a rag to his back, eh, Jack?"

JACK. *(Smiling)* "I'm black and blue all over from their fond caresses this afternoon."

EVELYN. *(Gaily)* "I'm off, then." *(Looking at Jack)* "You'll surely join us when we pass?"

JACK. "Sure thing."

EVELYN. *(Waving her hand)* "Bye-bye." *(She goes out. Jack sits down near his father.)*

TOWNSEND. *(Takes out a cigar and lights it. Jack watches him uneasily as if he foresees what his father is going to say and dreads it. Townsend avoids his eyes. There is an uncomfortable silence. Then Townsend begins vaguely)* "It certainly removes the burden of the years from my shoulders to come out to the old college in the Spring and live the old days over in memory and hobnob with some of the old-timers who were young-timers with me. It becomes more difficult every year I find. All the old landmarks are disappearing one by one."

JACK. *(Perfunctorily)* "Yes, even in my time there have been great changes."

TOWNSEND. *(Very palpably talking to gain time)* "It gives me a painful heart-throb every time I come back and look for some old place and find it renovated or torn down."

JACK. *(Shortly)* "I can well understand that."

TOWNSEND. "You don't realize what this college comes to mean to you in after years; how it becomes inseparably woven into the memories of one's lost youth until the two become identical."

JACK. *(Impatiently)* "Yes, I suppose so."

TOWNSEND. *(More and more vaguely)* "Happiest days of my life, of anyone's life - "

JACK. *(Abruptly)* "Come to the point, Dad."

TOWNSEND. *(Confused)* "What? Eh?"

JACK. *(Firmly)* "You didn't send Evelyn away in order that you might wax reminiscent; you know that, Dad."

TOWNSEND. *(Heaving a sigh of relief)* "You are quite right, I did not; but what I ought to speak about is such a deuced painful subject for both of us that I hardly dare speak of it - especially on your day of triumph when I should be the last one to bring up any unpleasantness."

JACK. *(Kindly)* "Never mind that, Dad."

TOWNSEND. "You see I didn't know when I'd have another opportunity of seeing you alone without arousing your mother's suspicions."

JACK. "I understand."

TOWNSEND. "And the thing has caused me so much worry. I simply had to hear from your own lips that everything was all right."

JACK. "Then I will set your mind at rest immediately. Everything *is* all right."

TOWNSEND. *(Fervently)* "Thank God for that! Why haven't you written to me?"

JACK. "Until a few days ago I had nothing new to tell you."

TOWNSEND. "When was the operation performed?"

JACK. "Last Monday."

TOWNSEND. "And you've heard from her since?"

JACK. "I received a short note from her that night. It was all over and everything was all right, she said. She told me I needn't worry any longer."

TOWNSEND. "That was five days ago. You haven't had any word since then?"

JACK. "No."

TOWNSEND. "That's a favorable sign. If any further complications had cropped up she would surely have let you know, wouldn't she?"

JACK. "Yes, I think she would. I imagine she's frightened to death and doesn't want any more to do with me. I'm sure I hope so. And then, you see I never answered her letter or telephoned."

TOWNSEND. *(Gravely)* "You were wrong there, my boy."

JACK *(Excitedly)* "I know it, I know it, Dad; but I had just received a letter from Evelyn telling me she was coming out for Commencement Week and the game, and - Oh, when I thought of her the other affair seemed so horrible and loathsome, I swore I'd never speak or write again. When I was certain she was in no danger I judged it best for both of us to break off once and for all."

TOWNSEND. "Listen, my boy; Are you sure - you know one's vanity blinds one in such cases - are you sure, absolutely sure, you were the father of this child which would have been born to her?"

JACK. *(Emphatically)* "Yes, I am certain of it, as certain as one can possibly be." *(Wildly)* "Oh I wish to God I had grounds for some suspicion of the sort. What a salve it would be for my conscience! But no, no! To even think such is an insult to a sweet girl." *(Defiantly)* "For she is a sweet, lovely girl in spite of everything, and if I had loved her the least particle, if I had not been in love with Evelyn, I should certainly have married her."

TOWNSEND. "Hm, - if you did not love this girl, why did you, - why, in the first place, - ?"

JACK. *(Leaning toward his father and fixing his eyes upon him searchingly)* "Why? Why? Who knows why or who, that does know, has the courage to confess it, even to himself. Be frank, Dad! Judging from several anecdotes which your friend Professor Simmons has let slip about your four years here, you were no St. Anthony. Turn your mind back to those days and then answer your own question: 'Why, in the first place?' "

TOWNSEND. *(Stares at the floor in moody retrospection - a pause)* "We've retained a large portion of the original mud in our make-up. That's the only answer I can think of."

JACK. *(Ironically)* "That's it! Do you suppose it was the same man who loves Evelyn who did this other thing? No, a thousand time no, such an idea is abhorrent. It was the male beast who ran gibbering through the forest after its female thousands of years ago."

TOWNSEND. "Come, Jack, that is pure evasion. You are responsible for the Mr. Hyde in you as well as for the Dr. Jekyll. Restraint - "

JACK. *(Scornfully)* "Restraint? Ah, yes, everybody preaches but who practices it? And could they if they wanted to? Some impulses are stronger than we are, have proved themselves so throughout the world's history. Is it not rather our ideals of conduct, of Right and Wrong, our ethics, which are unnatural and monstrously distorted? Is society not suffering from a case of the evil eye which sees evil where there is none? Isn't it our moral laws which force me into evasions like the one which you have just found fault with?"

TOWNSEND. "You're delving too deep, for me, my boy. Save your radical arguments for the younger generation. I cannot see them in the same light you do" *(Grumblingly)* "and if I could, I wouldn't. What I cannot understand is how you happened to get in with this young woman in the first place. You'll pardon me, Jack, but it seems to me to show a lack of judgment on your part, and - er - good taste."

JACK. *(Shrugging his shoulders)* "Such things usually are errors in taste."

TOWNSEND. "This young woman was hardly of the class you have been accustomed to associate with, I presume."

JACK. "She is a working girl, a stenographer."

TOWNSEND. "Has she any immediate relations who would be liable to discover the unfortunate termination of your" *(Sarcastically)* "Love affair?"

JACK. "Her father is dead. Her mother is a silly woman who would be the last to suspect anything. She has two sisters, both youngsters under ten, and one brother about eighteen, a machinist or something of the sort who is only home for weekends."

TOWNSEND. "And she and her brother support the others?"

JACK. *(Avoiding his father's eyes)* "So I believe."

TOWNSEND. *(His expression stern and accusing, starts to say something but restrains himself)* "Ah."

JACK. *(Glancing at his father)* "Yes, yes I know it, Dad. I have played the scoundrel all the way through. I realize that now. Why couldn't I have felt this way before, at the start? Then this would never have happened. But at that time the whole thing seemed just a pleasant game we were playing; its serious aspects appeared remote, unreal. I never gave them a thought. I have paid for it since then, I want you to believe that. I have had my glance into the abyss. In loss of confidence and self-respect, in bitter self-abasement I have paid, and I am sure the result of it all will be to make me a better man, a man more worthy to be Evelyn's husband."

TOWNSEND. *(Huskily)* "God grant it, my boy." *(Gets to his feet)* "I want to thank you for the confidence you placed in your father by making a frank appeal to me when you got in this trouble. It shows you regard me not only as a father but as a friend; and that is the way I would have it."

JACK. "You have always urged me to come to you and be frank about everything; and I always have and always will. I had to have the money and I thought I owed it to you to be open and aboveboard and not start in deceiving you at this late day. I couldn't get it in any other way very well. Two hundred dollars is quite a sum for a college student to raise at a moment's notice."

TOWNSEND. *(Restored to good humor)* "The wages of sin are rather exhorbitant."

JACK. "He was the only doctor I could find who would do that sort of thing. He knew I was a college student and probably made inquiries about your financial rating, - and there you are. There was nothing for me to do but grin and pay. But as I said in my letter this money is a loan. It would be unfair for me to make you shoulder my - mistakes."

TOWNSEND. *(Cheerfully)* "Let's forget all about it." *(He holds out his hand to Jack who clasps it heartily)* "All's well that ends well. You've learned your lesson." *(The sound of a college cheer comes faintly through the open window)* "And now shall we join the others? That cheer wakens the old fever in me. I want to follow the band and get singed by the Roman candles." *(He picks his straw hat from the table.)*

JACK. *(Eagerly)* "Yes, let's do that." *(They are going toward the door in the rear when Joe Murray appears in the doorway. Jack cannot repress an exclamation of alarm and his face grows pale.)*

MURRAY. *(Fixing his eyes on Jack with an expression of furious hatred)* "Look here, Townsend, I gotta see yuh for a minute."

JACK. *(Unwillingly)* "All right, Murray. You join the others, Dad, and I'll catch you in a few minutes." *(Townsend, struck by the change in his son's voice looks questioningly at him, asking an explanation. Jack turns away from him.)*

JACK. "Come in, Murray, and have a seat." *(Townsend goes out. Murray slouches to the middle of the room but does not sit down. His fingers fumble nervously at the buttons of his coat. He notices this and plunges his hands into his coat pockets. He seems endeavoring to restrain the hatred and rage which the spasmodic working of his features show to be boiling within him.)*

JACK. *(Appears occupied in arranging the things on the table)* "Well?"

MURRAY. *(Chokingly)* "Well!" *(He can go no further.)*

JACK *(Coldly, without looking at him)* "Anything I can do for you?"

MURRAY. *(In strangled tones)* "Anything you can do for me!"

JACK. *(Hurriedly)* "Yes; I'm in rather a hurry and if it's nothing very important I'd be just as well pleased if you'd come some other time."

MURRAY. "Important? *You* mayn't think so. It's not important to *you*, yuh -" *(He is stopped by a fit of violent coughing which racks his thin body.)*

JACK. *(Irritably)* "You've come here looking for trouble, Murray. You better wait until you've cooled off." *(Then more kindly)* "What is it you want to say to me? Out with it!"

MURRAY. *(Wiping his mouth on his coat sleeve - angrily)* "I'll out with it, damn yuh! - standing there so cool - dressed in swell clothes - and all these other goils -" *(Choking)* "and Nellie - and Nellie - "

JACK. *(Leaning toward him)* "Yes, Nellie?"

MURRAY *(Sobbing)* "She's dead." *(In a transport of rage)* "*You* killed her, yuh dirty murderer!"

JACK. *(Dully, as if he did not understand)* "Dead? No, no, you don't mean that. She wrote to me everything was all right. Dead?" *(As he speaks he backs away from Murray in horror and stumbles against one of the Morris chairs. He sits down in it mechanically.)*

MURRAY. *(Shrilly)* "She's dead - Nellie, my sister - she's dead."

JACK. *(Half to himself)* "No, it's impossible." *(Fiercely)* "It's a lie! What scheme is this of yours? You're trying to frighten me."

MURRAY. *(Raging)* "She's dead, I tell yuh, dead! She died this morning."

JACK. *(Forced to believe)* "She died this morning?" *(In a dazed voice)* "But why didn't she - I didn't know -" *(Stares straight before him)* "God!"

MURRAY. "Why didn't she let yuh know, yuh mean? She wrote to yuh, she told me she did; and yuh knew she was sick and never answered it. She might'a lived if she thought yuh cared, if she heard from yuh; but she knew yuh were tryin' to git rid of her."

JACK. *(In agony)* "Stop, for God's sake! I know I should have written. I meant to write but - "

MURRAY. "She kept sayin': 'I wanta die. I don't wanta live!' " *(Furiously)* "But I'll fix yuh! I'll make yuh pay."

JACK. *(Startled, turns to him quickly)* "What do you mean?"

MURRAY. "Don't give me any of that. Yuh know what I mean. Yuh know how she died." *(Fiercely)* "Yuh know who killed her."

JACK. *(His voice trembling - not looking at Murray)* "How she died? Killed her? I don't understand - "

MURRAY. "Yuh lie! She was murdered and yuh know it."

JACK. *(Horror-struck)* "Murdered?"

MURRAY. "Yes, and *you* murdered her."

JACK. *(Shuddering)* "I? What? I murdered? - Are you crazy?"

MURRAY. "You and your dirty skunk of a doctor."

JACK. *(Sinks back in his chair with a groan)* "Ooh!"

MURRAY. *(With fierce scorn)* "Yuh thought yuh was safe, didn't yuh, with me away from home? Yuh c'd go out and pitch the champeenship game - and she lyin' dead! Yuh c'd ruin her and throw her down and no one say a word because yuh're a swell college guy and captain of the team, and she ain't good enough for yuh to marry. She's goin' to have a kid, *your* kid, and because yuh're too rotten to act like a man, yuh send her to a

faker of a doctor to be killed; and she does what yuh say because
she loves yuh; and yuh don't even think enough of her to answer her letter" (*Sobbing*) "when she's dyin' on account of
you!"

JACK. (*Speaking with difficulty*) "She - told you - all this?"

MURRAY. "Not a word!" (*Proudly*) "She died game; she
wasn't no coward. I tried every way I knew how to git her to
tell me but she wouldn't. Not a word outa her against you."
(*Choking with angry sobs*) "And *you* - and *you* - yuh dirty
coward! - playin' ball!"

JACK. (*Dully*) "I did what I thought was best for her."

MURRAY. "Yuh sneaked out like a coward because yuh thought
she wasn't good enough." (*With a sneer*) "Yuh think yuh c'n
get away with that stuff and then marry some goil of your
own kind, I s'pose, - some goil like I seen yuh come in with
tonight." (*Vindictively*) "But yuh won't; not if I have to go to
hell for it!" (*A pause. Jack is silent, breathing hard. His eyes
are haunted, full of despair, as he vainly seeks to escape from the
remorse which is torturing him. The faint sound of the college
cheer, then of the band, comes from the open window. From
this point to the end these sounds are continuous, the band only
being silenced to permit the giving of the cheer, and as the action
progresses they become more and more distinct.*)

MURRAY. (*Continues in the same vindictive tones*) "I've always hated yuh since yuh first come to the house. I've always
hated all your kind. Yuh come here to school and yuh think yuh
c'n do as yuh please with us town people. Yuh treat us like servants, an' what are *you*, I'd like to know? - a lot of lazy no-good
dudes spongin' on your old men; and the goils, our goils, think
yuh're grand!" (*Jack is staring at the floor, his head bowed, and
does not seem to hear him.*)

MURRAY. "I knew somethin' would happen. I told Nellie to look out, and she laughed. When the old lady sent for me and I come home and saw Nellie and she wouldn't leave me go for a doctor, I had a hunch what was wrong. She wouldn't say nothin' but I got our doc, not the one *you* sent her to, and he told me just what I thought and said she was goin' to die." (*Raging*) "If I'd seen yuh that minute I'd killed yuh. I knew it was *you* but I couldn't prove it. Then one of the kids got scared and told me Nellie'd sent her to your doc for medicine when she first took sick. I bought a gun and the kid showed me where he was. I shoved the gun in his face and he owned up and told me about you. He offered me money, lots of it, to keep my mouth shut, and I took it - the money he'd got from you - blood money!" (*With a savage grin*) "An' I'll keep my mouth shut - maybe!"

JACK. (*His eyes lighting up with a gleam of hope, turns eagerly to Murray*) "Listen, Murray! This affair is unspeakably horrible, and I am - everything you say; but I want you - you must believe I honestly thought I was acting for the best in having the operation performed. That it has turned out so tragically is terrible. You cannot realize how I am suffering. I feel as if I were what you called me - a murderer." (*Brokenly*) "It is horrible, horrible! The thought of it will torture me all my life."

MURRAY. "That don't bring her back to life. Yuh're too late!"

JACK. (*Frenziedly*) "Too late! What do you mean? You haven't told anyone? You haven't - "

MURRAY. "When I left his office I went home and - she was dead. Then I come up here lookin' for *you*. I wanted to kill yuh, but - I been thinkin' - yuh're not worth gittin' hung for." (*With a cruel grin*) "I c'n see a better way of fixin' yuh, - one that'll get yuh right."

JACK. *(Half to himself)* "You haven't told anyone?"

MURRAY. "What's the difference? There's plenty of time. *I* know."

JACK. *(Trying to steady his voice which is trembling with apprehension)* "Murray, for your own sake, for your dead sister's good name, for your family's sake you must keep this thing quiet. I do not plead for myself. I am willing to have you punish me individually in any way you see fit; but there are others, innocent ones, who will suffer."

MURRAY. "She was innocent, too, before you - "

JACK. *(Interrupting him)* "My mother and father, my sister, Ev -" *(Bites back the name)* "This would kill my mother if she knew. They are innocent. Do not revenge yourself on them."

MURRAY. *(Inflexibly)* "You killed my sister."

JACK. "Why will you keep saying that? You know it was an accident; that I would gladly have given my own life rather than have it happen. And you must keep silent. I will do anything you want, I tell you!" *(He goes close to Murray)* "You say the doctor gave you money? I'll give you ten times as much as he did." *(Murray's face grows livid)* "I'll see that you get so much a year for the rest of your life. My father is rich. We'll get you a good position, do everything you wish," *(Breaking down)* "only do not punish the innocent."

MURRAY. *(Slowly)* "You want - to pay me - for Nellie!" *(With a terrible cry of rage he pulls a revolver from the pocket of his coat. Before he can pull the trigger Jack seizes his wrist. There is a short struggle. Jack takes the revolver away from him and lays it on the table. Murray has a violent attack of coughing. He recovers and is slinking toward the door when Jack suddenly picks up the revolver from the table and holds it out to him.)*

JACK. *(Steadily)* "Here, take it! I was a fool to stop you. Let the thing end with me and leave the innocent alone."

MURRAY. *(Malevolently)* "It's too good for yuh." *(He has edged stealthily nearer and nearer the door and with a final spring gains the safety of the dark hallway. He shouts back)* "I'm goin' to the p'lice station. D'yuh hear, yuh dirty ba - rd! To the p'lice station!" *(His quick footsteps can be heard as he runs out. Jack makes a movement as if to follow him but stops and sits down heavily by the table, laying the revolver on it. He hears the band and the cheers of the paraders who have evidently just invaded that section of the campus. He hurries to the windows, closes them, and pulls down the shades. The band is playing a march song and the students are singing. Jack groans and hides his face in his hands. The parade is about to pass by his windows. The glare of the red fire glows dully on the window shades. Jack springs up and rushes into his bedroom on the right. Several students crowd in the doorway from the hall.)*

ONE STUDENT. "He's not here."

ANOTHER STUDENT. "He ran away." *(All go out laughing and shouting. The band stops playing. Jack comes out from the bedroom, his face drawn with agony. The cheerleader's voice can be heard shouting)* "He ran away but if we give him a cheer, he'll hear us. A long cheer for Townsend, fellows! Hip! Hip!" *(Jack staggers toward the window crying brokenly)* "No! No! For God's sake!" *(The first part of the cheer booms out. He reels to the table and sees the revolver lying there. He snatches it up and presses it to his temple. The report is drowned by the cheering. He falls forward on his face, twiches, is still.)*

THE STUDENTS. *(Winding up the nine long rahs)* "Rah! Rah! Rah! Townsend! Townsend! Townsend!" *(The band strikes up: "For He's A Jolly Good Fellow." The students com-*

mence to sing. The parade moves off again. Evelyn appears in the doorway to the rear.)

EVELYN. "Jack! It's all right now, dear. You can come out of hiding." *(She blinks for a moment blinded by the light; then comes into the room and sees the body - in terror)* "Jack! What's the matter?" *(She rushes over and kneels beside him; then faints as she sees the blood on his temples, the revolver still clutched in his right hand. She falls on the floor beside him.)*

THE STUDENTS. *(Their voices growing gradually fainter)* "For he's a jolly good fellow, which nobody can deny."

THE CURTAIN FALLS

"THE MOVIE MAN" (1914)

A Comedy In One Act

CHARACTERS

HENRY (HEN) ROGERS, *Representative of
Earth Motion Picture Company.*

AL DEVLIN, *Photographer for the same Company.*

PANCHO GOMEZ, *Commander-in-Chief
of the Constitutionalist Army.*

LUIS VIRELLA, *General of Division.*

ANITA FERNANDEZ.

A SENTRY.

SCENE: *The main room of a house in the suburb of a large town in northern Mexico. To the left, a whitewashed wall of adobe with a small black crucifix hanging from a nail. In the rear wall, a doorway opening on the street. On either side of the doorway, an open window. On the right side of the room, another door which is closed. On the wall above it, a faded lithograph of the Virgin. In the left-hand corner several Mauser carbines are stacked, and bandoleers of cartridges are thrown on the dirt floor beside them. In the right-hand corner several saddles are lying. Near the door, another saddle. In the middle of the room a rickety table with a pen, paper, and ink on it. Three or four stiff cane-bottomed chairs are placed about the table.*

Hen Rogers and Al Devlin are sitting by the table. Both are smoking pipes. Both are dressed in khaki shirts, riding breeches, puttees, etc. Their wide-brimmed Stetson hats are on the table beside them. Rogers is tall, blond, clean-shaven, in his early thirties. Devlin is short, dark, with a good-natured irregular face, middle-aged.

A sentry in a filthy, ragged olive-drab uniform lolls in the doorway leaning on his rifle. He wears the wide sombrero of the Mexican peon, and is bare-footed. He is smoking a cigarette and watching the two Americans with an expression of bored indifference.

It is in the early hours of a sultry tropic night.

DEVLIN. (*Singing in a cracked falsetto*) "Mexico, my nice cool Mexico!"

ROGERS. (*Mopping the perspiration from his forehead with a bandana handkerchief.*) "Have a heart, Al, have a heart, and kill the canary-bird stuff. If you see anything to be merry over in this flea-bitten cluster of shanties, you got something on me."

DEVLIN. (*Chuckling*) "Lovely little spot to spend the summer!"

ROGERS. (*Dryly*) "Ideal is the word. And speaking of fleas, on the level, I never knew what a poor dog has to put up with until I hit this one-horse country."

DEVLIN. "They don't bother me any."

ROGERS. "No, they've got some class, you gotta hand it to them."

DEVLIN. "Is *that* so?"

ROGERS. " 'Discretion is the better part of valor' - any well-bred Mexican flea is hep to that. Those are the first words in the Mexican Constitution and every man and beast in this country swears by them; if they didn't we'd have been in Mexico City months ago; and right now I'd be down at Manhattan Beach in God's Country with a large mint julep, full of ice - "

DEVLIN. (*With a groan*) "Help! Help! I'm a nut!"

ROGERS. "When this cruel war is over and on the films I'm going to quit the picture business and go way up north, marry an Esquimau, and start housekeeping on an exclusive, refined, accordion-pleated, little iceberg."

DEVLIN. (*Whistles shrilly to the sentry who grabs his rifle in alarm.*) "Boy, page an iceberg for Mr. Rogers!"

THE SENTRY. (*With lazy scorn.*) "Muy loco!"

ROGERS. "What's that he said, Al? Look it up in your little book. It sounded almost like real talk."

DEVLIN. (*With a laugh.*) "I don't have to look that up. He means we're crazy."

ROGERS. (*To the sentry - approvingly.*) "You said something then, Mike. We sure are as nutty as a fruitcake or we wouldn't be here. Phew, but it's hot!" (*After a short pause musingly*) "Say, Al, did you ever notice the happy, contented expression on a polar bear's face?"

DEVLIN. (*Laughing*) "Basta! Basta!" (*The sentry instinctively springs to attention, then lapses into indifference again as he realizes it is only the crazy American speaking.*)

ROGERS. "Say, you're getting to be a regular talker of spigoty! Slip me the answer to that word 'basta', will you? I hear friend General pulling it all the time; and just to show you what a fine little guesser I am, I'll bet you a case-note it means 'when'."

DEVLIN. "Come across with that peso. It doesn't mean 'when'; it means 'enough'."

ROGERS. "Same thing - I knew it - I never yet heard him say it when I was pouring him out a drink."

DEVLIN. "You owe me a peso, don't forget it."

ROGERS. (*Grumblingly*) "I'm not liable to with you around." (*An excited babble of voices is heard from the door on the right*) "Listen to those boobs, will you! What do you suppose they're framing up in there?"

DEVLIN. "Who is it - Gomez?"

ROGERS. "Yes; he and all his little generals are having some sort of a confab. I'll bet you that smack back again he's going to try and capture the town tomorrow."

DEVLIN. "What's this you're springing on me - inside information?"

ROGERS. "Nope; but this afternoon I gave him that case of Scotch I promised him when he signed our contract, and he's feeling some brave this evening."

DEVLIN. "Say, Hen, about that contract, I forgot to tell you, you wanta hand a call to this Gomez guy. He is playing the game. You remember the other day when they were going after that fort on the outskirts?"

ROGERS. "Sure - good stuff - plenty of real live action that day."

DEVLIN. (*Indignantly*) "It was good stuff all right, but I missed all the first part of it on account of that simp General Virella. He was just waving his sword and ordering 'em to charge when I came up. 'Here you!' I said to him, 'wait a minute. Can't you see I'm not ready for you yet?' And what do you think that greaser said to me? You know he speaks good English. He says: 'Shall my glorious soldiers be massacred waiting for your machine?' And away he runs with all his yellow-bellies after him. What d'you know about that?"

ROGERS. (*Frowning*) "He's a fresh guy, that Virella. I'll have Gomez stick him back in the rear after this. He's a mean little worm, too. He's the one who's nagged Gomez into croaking old Fernandez."

DEVLIN. "What! Are they going to shoot Fernandez?"

ROGERS. "At sunrise tomorrow they stand him against the wall and - curtain."

DEVLIN. "It's a damn shame - just because they can't get any more coin out of him. He's a good fellow - Fernandez. Went to school in the States - Cornell or someplace. Can't you get him off?"

ROGERS. "Nix. Virella has a grudge against him and Gomez needs Virella. Anyway, I've got no license to butt in on their little scraps. Besides it'll make a great picture. Be sure and get it."

DEVLIN. "I'll be there. Say, have them hold it till a little later, will you? The light isn't any good so early."

ROGERS. "How'll eight o'clock do?"

DEVLIN. "Great!"

ROGERS. "All right, I'll tell Gomez to postpone it till then." (*A shrill voice is heard shouting: 'Viva' from the room on the right.*) "That's Virella, now. I'd like to take just one swing at that guy. They'd carry him home in a white-pine kimona." (*Another cheer from the room next door*) "Full of booze and patriotism! Gee, I wish I was a war correspondent. I'd send in a little notice like this: 'The courage and spirits of the troops were never better. A trainload of rum arrived today. We will be in Mexico City in two weeks'."

DEVLIN. (*Picking his hat from the table, gets to his feet.*) "I think I'll take a look around and see what's doing."

ROGERS. "Oho! I've got your number all right!"

DEVLIN. (*Laughing*) "What do you mean: got my number?"

ROGERS. "Have a care, little one, have a care! Some one of these Mexican dolls you're googooing at will carve her initials on your back with the breadknife some one of these days."

DEVLIN. "I should fret!"

ROGERS. (*Disgustedly*) "What you can see in these skirts, has got me beat. They're so homely the mules shy at them."

DEVLIN. "Is *that* so? Well, let me tell you, there's some class to some of the dames down here. You ought to have seen the bear I lamped this afternoon. Some queen, take it from me."

ROGERS. "Load that noise in one of the cannons and fire it off!"

DEVLIN. "On the level, Hen, she had the swellest lamps I've ever seen on a dame; and a figure - my boy! my boy!"

ROGERS. "Captain Sweeney of the Marines, please listen! And I suppose you copped her and dated her up?"

DEVLIN. "Nothing like it, Hen. She was doing a sob act on one of the benches in that little park out here, and I asked her in my best Spanish what was the matter. Phew! Talk about the icy once-over! She looked at me as if I was a wet dog. I turned and beat it like a little man."

ROGERS. "You were wise, for once. She'd have operated on you with her stiletto in another second. I wouldn't trust one of these dolls as far as I could hit Walter Johnson's fast one."

DEVLIN. "But what d'you suppose she was doing a weep about?"

ROGERS. (*Dryly*) "Maybe one of her husbands got killed in the war."

DEVLIN. "What sweet thoughts you have! S'long, Hen. Don't forget to have Gomez postpone that shooting thing." (*He goes to door in rear.*)

ROGERS. "I won't; and you come back early - if you're still alive. I want you to scratch my back before I hit the hay. I'd have to be a contortionist or a centipede to follow this flea-game properly."

DEVLIN. (*Laughing*) "They'll take your mind off your worries. Be good!" (*He passes the sentry and disappears in the darkness. Another cheer is heard from the next room. Rogers grunts disgustedly and attempts to scratch the middle of his back. The sentry's head falls forward on his chest as he dozes in the doorway.*

Anita Fernandez appears outside the door and creeps stealthily by the sentry into the room. She is a beautiful young Mexican girl with a mass of black hair and great black eyes. She stumbles over the saddle by the door and utters a little cry of pain. The sentry wakes up, rushes over to her and grabs her furiously by the arm. He drags her toward the door. Rogers springs from his chair and yells at the sentry.)

ROGERS. "Hey, you Mike, what are you doing? Let go of that dame!" (*The sentry scowls uncertainly at him. Rogers makes a threatening gesture and the sentry releases Anita and returns to his post by the doorway. Anita sinks into a chair by the table and, hiding her face in her hands, commences to sob. Rogers stands beside not knowing what to do.*)

ROGERS. "What'll I say to her?" (*Sees the English-Spanish book of Devlin's on the table.*) "Here's Al's Spanish book. Let's see." (*Turns over the pages.*) "What do you want? - I wonder how you say it - Oh, here it is." (*He repeats the line to himself, then bends down to Anita.*) "Que quere, Senorita?" (*He pro-*

nounces it 'Kwi query, Seenorita?' She raises her head and stares at him with a puzzled expression.) "She doesn't make me at all - Oh Hell!"

ANITA. *(Haughtily)* "Pleese to not swear, senor."

ROGERS. *(Confused)* "Excuse me - awfully sorry - tongue slipped." *(With a sigh of relief)* "Thank Go - heavens, you speak English."

ANITA. "But most badly, senor."

ROGERS. *(Sitting down across the table from her)* "No, very good, just as good as mine. Who was it you wanted to see?"

ANITA. "El Generalissimo Gomez."

ROGERS. *(Shaking his head)* "You better wait. He'll be all lit up like a torch tonight."

ANITA. *(Mystified)* "Senor?"

ROGERS. "You know what I mean - he's soused, pickled, stewed, boiled -"

ANITA. *(In puzzled accents)* "Es-stewed? Boiled?" *(In horrified tones)* "You mean he is cooking - the General? But no, senor, I onderstand Eenglish veree badly. For one year alone, I estudy in the convent in Nueva York - Noo York. Then mi madre - my mothair - die and I must come home to the house of my fathair becose I have more years - I am older than my sisters." *(There is a ringing "Viva" from the next room. Anita turns pale.)*

ROGERS. *(Making a motion with his hand as if he were taking a drink and nodding toward the room.)* "You understand now? He's drinking, and -"

ANITA. *(Shuddering)* "Ah, he es drunk, no?"

ROGERS. "I'm afraid he will be before he leaves that room - if he isn't already."

ANITA. (*The tears starting to her eyes*) "Mi padre!"

ROGERS. "You better wait until tomorrow to see him."

ANITA. "Eet ees not possible. I must - tonight!"

ROGERS. (*Earnestly*) "Don't do it, Kid! Don't you know Gomez is a bad guy - man - for a young girl to come and see at night - 'specially when he's drunk?"

ANITA. (*Flushing*) "I know, si, senor, but eet must be."

ROGERS. "Won't you tell me why?"

ANITA. (*Her voice trembling*) "Si, I will tell you. Eet ees not long to tell, senor. You have heard - you know Ernesto Fernandez?"

ROGERS. "You mean the Fernandez who is going to be shot tomorrow morning?"

ANITA. (*Shuddering*) "Si, senor, he eet ees I mean. He ees my fathair."

ROGERS. (*Astounded*) "Your father! Good God!"

ANITA. "I must see the General Gomez tonight to ask him to save my fathair."

ROGERS. "He will not do it."

ANITA. (*Faintly*) "You know that, senor?"

ROGERS. "Virella is with him - in there - now!"

ANITA. (*Terrified*) "Virella? He is the most bad enemy of my fathair."

ROGERS. "You might buy Gomez off; pay him to set your father free. He'll do anything for money. Have you any money?"

ANITA. "Alas, no, senor; Gomez has taken from us everything."

ROGERS. "Too bad, too bad! Hm - Well, you mustn't stay

here any longer. They're liable to come out any minute. Go home now, and I'll see what I can do with Gomez."

ANITA. (*Resolutely*) "Gracias, I thank you, senor; you are very kind - but I must see Gomez."

ROGERS. (*Deliberately, - looking steadily into her eyes*) "Don't you know what Gomez will want - the price he will make you pay if he finds you here?"

ANITA. (*Closing her eyes and swaying weakly on her feet*) "For the life - of my fathair - " (*Sobs softly*)

ROGERS. (*Looking at her in admiration*) "God!"

ANITA. (*Fiercely*) "I would keel myself to save him!"

ROGERS. "But even if he said he'd free your father you couldn't believe him. What is Gomez' word worth? No, you must let me fix this for you."

ANITA. (*Doubtfully*) "But you - Gomez ees veree powerful, senor - ees it possible for you to do?"

ROGERS. (*Decisively*) "I'll save your old man if I have to start a revolution of my own to do it."

ANITA. (*Her eyes shining with gratitude*) "Ah, thank you, senor - but if you should fail?"

ROGERS. (*Emphatically*) "I won't fail. You just watch me start something!" (*He has scarcely finished speaking when the door to the right is thrown open and Gomez and Virella enter the room. They are both in a state of great excitement and show they have been drinking. Virella is an undersized man with shifty, beady black eyes and a black mustache. Gomez is tall and heavily built with a bloated dissipated-looking face and a bristly black mustache. Both are dressed in new uniforms of olive-drab and wear military caps. Cartridge-belts with automatic revolvers in leather holsters are strapped about their waists over their coats.*

*Anita stares at them for a moment with horrified loathing;
then shrinks away into the far corner of the room. Gomez turns
to shout an "Adios" to the officers who are still carousing in
the room he has just left; then bangs the door shut behind him.
Virella sees Anita and walks toward her with a drunken leer on
on his flushed face.)*

VIRELLA. "Buenos noches, senorita."

ROGERS. (*Steps forward and places himself in front of Virella
whom he grasps by the shoulders and forcibly turns in the direction of the door.)* "Now, beat it, Snake-in-the-Grass!"

VIRELLA. (*Struggling to free himself*) "Pig of a Gringo!"

ROGERS. "General Gomez and I want to have a talk in private,
don't we, Gomez?" (*He glances at Gomez with a command-
ing air.*)

GOMEZ. (*Uncertainly*) "Por cierto, amigo, if you like eet."

VIRELLA. (*Frothing at the mouth with rage*) "Dog! Pig!"

ROGERS. (*Calmly*) "Those are hard words, my pet - and you
hear what your general commands?" (*He turns to Gomez.*)

GOMEZ. "Si, Virella, I command eet."

ROGERS. (*To Virella, contemptuously*) "Now blow before I
crown you!" (*He draws back his fist threateningly. Virella
shrinks away from him, salutes Gomez, and slinks out of the
door in rear.*)

GOMEZ. (*Forcing a laugh*) "Ees thees the way you treat my
generals?"

ROGERS. "You ought to shoot that little scorpion - before he
shoots you."

GOMEZ (*Frowning*) "Eet ees true, amigo, what you say, and
pairhaps soon - but - now he ees to me necessary." (*He notices
Anita for the first time and turns to Rogers with a chuckle.*) "Ex-

cuse me, a senorita!" (*Takes his cap off and makes her a gallant bow*) "Ah, Senior Rogers, you are - how you call eet? - a man of - ladies, no?" (*He walks over to Anita who shrinks back to the wall in terror.*) "Have you fear of me, chiquita? Of Gomez? But Pancho Gomez, he loav the ladies, that ees well known. Ask el senor Rogers." (*He chucks her under the chin.*)

ROGERS. (*Stepping between them - quietly*) "This young lady is *my* friend, Gomez."

GOMEZ. (*Biting his lips*) "I say in fun only." (*He walks back to the table and remarks sullenly to Rogers who is following him.*) "She ees 'muy hermosa', veree preety, your senorita."

ROGERS. "She is the daughter of Ernesto Fernandez."

GOMEZ. (*Surprised*) "Que dice? What you say?"

ROGERS. "She's the daughter of the man you're going to have shot in the morning. She came to ask you - "

GOMEZ. (*Emphatically*) "No, hombre, no! I know what you will say. I can not do. Eet ees not possible!" (*Anita rushes forward and throws herself at his feet.*) "No, no, no, senorita, I must go." (*He strides toward the door in the rear. Anita lies where she has thrown herself, sobbing hopelessly.*)

ROGERS. "One minute, Gomez! Where are you going?"

GOMEZ. "To prepare the attack. Ah, I forget! I have not tole you." (*Excitedly*) "Tonight, amigo, we storm the town. We catch them asleep, no? and before they wake they are - " (*He makes a motion across his neck with his forefinger.*) "dead, how you call eet? - as a nail." (*Proudly*) "Eet ees a plan sublime, most glorious - eet ees the plan of Gomez! In one small week, hombre, shall we be in Mexico City."

ROGERS. "That Scotch is great stuff. One more drink and old Napoleon would be a piker."

GOMEZ. (*Puzzled*) "What you say?"

ROGERS. "Nothing, nothing." (*His face lighting up with a ray of hope.*) "A night attack, eh?"

GOMEZ. "Si, hombre, at twelve hours - twelve o'clock."

ROGERS. (*Calmly*) "Who said so?"

GOMEZ. "I say it, I, Pancho Gomez!"

ROGERS. (*Emphatically*) "Well, you just listen to me, Gomez; I say you can't do it. There'll be no night attacks in this war when I'm around." (*Gomez is stupefied*) "How do you expect us to get pictures at night? You didn't think of that, eh?"

GOMEZ. (*Bewildered*) "But, amigo -"

ROGERS. "Nix on the night attacks, do you get me?" (*Pulls a paper out of his pocket.*) "Here's a copy of your contract giving us rights to all your fights *all*, do you hear, all! And we got one clause especially for night attacks." (*Reads*) "The party of the second part hereby agrees to fight no battles at night or on rainy days or at any time whatsoever when the light is so poor as to make the taking of motion pictures impracticable. Failure to comply with these conditions will constitute a breach of contract and free the party of the first part from all the obligations entered into by this contract." (*Hands the contract to Gomez.*) "Here it is, black and white, English and Spanish both, with your signature at the bottom with mine. Read for yourself." (*Gomez glances at the paper mechanically and hands it back.*)

GOMEZ. (*With a defiant snarl*) "And if I say: 'To hell, you!' Then what you do, eh?"

ROGERS. (*Mimicking the General's tone*) "Who buys and sends you most of your ammunition, eh? Who pays you and the other Generals and the German in charge of your artillery - the only man who savvys how to use the guns right - eh? Who has promised to see that you get siege guns for Mexico City and twenty more machine guns with men, real men, to run them for you, eh? Your soldiers'll desert you if you don't pay them soon, and you know it. Well, who has agreed to loan you the money to give them their back pay, eh? And, above all, who has promised to help you become President when you reach Mexico City?" (*Impressively*) "We have - The Earth Motion Picture Company! Well, you break this contract and all that stops, see? and goes to the other side."

GOMEZ. (*Softly - fingering his revolver*) "Bueno; but I can also have you shot, hombre."

ROGERS. "Nix on that rough stuff! You wouldn't dare. You've got to keep on the right side of the U.S.A. or your revolution isn't worth the powder to blow it to - Mexico."

GOMEZ. (*Pleadingly*) "But, amigo, permit eet this once. The plan is fine, the town will be ours, my soldiers will steal and no more grumble against Gomez. Tomorrow I will shoot all the prisoners for your pictures, I promise eet."

ROGERS. (*Kindly*) "I'd like to do you a favor, Gomez, but I don't see my way to do this, unless - "

GOMEZ. (*With a smile*) "Aha, tell me, hombre, your price."

ROGERS. (*Firmly*) "The life of Ernesto Fernandez!" (*Anita jumps to her feet and stretches out her arms beseechingly to Gomez. He twirls his mustache thoughtfully for a moment.*)

GOMEZ. "Bueno, my friend, I accept your terms." (*He goes to the table and hurriedly scratches a few lines which he hands to Anita.*) "Su padre de uste - your father, he ees free, senorita. For this thank my fine friend Senor Rogers." (*He claps Rogers jovially on the back.*) "Now must I have shot the General Virella who will never forgive me your father should live, senorita. Mexico ees too es-small for those two hombres - both alive."

(*Pulls a flask from his pocket and offers it to Rogers who refuses with a smile.*) "Senor Rogers - how you call eet? - here ees looking at you!" (*Drinks*) "And now I must to prepare the attack." (*Goes to the door; then turns and remarks grandiloquently*) "Should anyone wish me, senor, tell them that een the hour of battle, Pancho Gomez, like the immortal Juarez, will ever be found at the head of his brave soldiers. Adios!" (*He makes a sweeping bow and goes out past the saluting sentry.*)

ROGERS. (*With a long whistle of amusement - turning to Anita*) "Some bull! Honest, you've got to hand it to that guy, at that."

ANITA. "And now I, too, must go - to my poor fathair."

ROGERS. "Can't I take you there? You know there's lots of drunken soldiers around and - "

ANITA. "No, no, senor, you are too kind. Eet ees but two steps to the carcel - the prison. Eet ees not necessary." (*Indicating the paper in her hand*) "The name of Gomez is most sufficient." (*Holding out her hand to him with a shy smile*) "Muchissima gracias, senor, - with all my heart do I thank you. My fathair and I - we will be at the home tomorrow - eet ees the first hacienda beyond the hill - you will come, senor? As a brother, my father's son, shall you be to us!"

ROGERS. (*Holding her hand and looking into her eyes*) "Only - a brother?"

ANITA. (*Drawing her hand away in confusion, runs to the door; then turns*) "Quien sabe, senor? Who knows?" (*She hurries out.*)

ROGERS. (*Does a few Spanish dance steps, snapping his fingers and humming. The sentry grins at him.*) "What are you grinning at, Mike?"

THE SENTRY. (*With a contemptuous smile makes a gesture of turning a wheel near his head*) "Muy loco!"

ROGERS. "I got you the first time, Mike. Crazy is the right word." (*He commences to sing*) "Mexico, My bright-eyed Mexico." (*Devlin appears in the doorway and scowls darkly at him.*)

DEVLIN. "Kill it, kill it, you bone!" (*Comes in and throws his hat irritably on the table. Rogers looks at him with an amused smile.*) "What're you chirping about? Are you soused, too? Where have you hidden the joy-water? Everyone in this bush-league army seems all corned up tonight except me. Say I just got another flash at that dame I was telling you about. She looked right through me at something behind my back. Some nerve to that greaser chicken giving a real white man the foot!" (*Scornfully*) "I got a good slant at her this time. She isn't much to look at after all. Back in God's Country we'd use her photo for a before-taking ad."

ROGERS. (*Indignantly*) "Al, you always were a simp!" (*Grumblingly*) "Better get a pair of cheaters for those bum lamps of yours." (*Cheerfully*) "Cheer up, Al, you're all wrong, my son, you're all wrong!" (*Devlin gapes at him in open-mouthed amazement, Rogers commences to sing again: "Mexico, my bright-eyed Mexico." The sentry grunts contemptuously, as*

THE CURTAIN FALLS

"THE SNIPER" (1915)

A Play In One Act

CHARACTERS

ROUGON, *a Belgian peasant.*

THE VILLAGE PRIEST.

A GERMAN CAPTAIN OF INFANTRY.

FOUR PRIVATES OF THE REGIMENT.

JEAN, *a peasant boy.*

SCENE: *The main room of a ruined cottage on the outskirts of a small Belgian village. The rear wall has two enormous breaches made by the shells of the artillery. The right wall is partly hidden by a mass of wreckage from the roof, which has caved in leaving a jagged hole through which the sky can be seen. The ceiling slants drunkenly downward toward the right, ending abruptly in a ragged edge of splintered boards and beams which forms a fantastic fretwork against the sky. The floor is littered with all kinds of debris.*

In the rear wall near the right corner, a window, its panes of glass all broken, with a torn white curtain. No trace of the doorway to the road remains. The larger breach in the rear wall is used as exit and entrance.

The left wall, with a door in the middle, is uninjured. Over the door a large black crucifix hangs from a nail.

In the center of the room, an overturned table. A solitary chair, the only thing left standing, is beside it. On the right of the table a smashed armchair.

The time is about sundown on a September day. Through the breaches in the wall a dark green vista of rolling fields can be seen. Where they meet the horizon they are already shimmering in the golden dust of the sunset. Muffled and far-off, the booming of distant cannon reverberates slowly over the fields.

The sound of shuffling footsteps is heard from the road before the cottage and a great hulking old man of sixty-five or so appears at the larger breach in the rear wall. He is dressed in the usual peasant fashion and wears wooden sabots on his feet. He is bent under some burden which, as he enters the room, is seen to be the body of a young man dressed in the uniform of a Belgian infantryman. He lays the body down carefully in a cleared space between the table and the left wall, pillowing the soldier's head upon his knapsack. The body lies with its feet toward the rear wall.

He stands looking down at the still form, his attitude one of abject despair. A heavy sob shakes his round shoulders. He murmurs brokenly; "Charles! My little one!"; then turns abruptly and stumbles to the middle of the room where he mechanically rights the overturned table. He sits down on the chair, and stares at the ruins about him with an expression of dazed bewilderment on his broad face, his round, child-like eyes wandering dully from one object to another. His gaze finally rests on the smashed armchair on the other side of the table, and suddenly overcome by a flood of anguished horror, he hides his face in his hands, rocking from side to side on his chair, moaning to himself like a wounded animal.

The slight black-robed figure of a priest appears on the road outside. He casts a quick glance into the room and, seeing the bowed figure on the chair quickly picks his way to the peasant's side. The priest is old, white-haired, with a kindly, spiritual face.

THE PRIEST. "Rougon!"

ROUGON. (*Not hearing him*) "God, oh God!"

THE PRIEST. (*Laying a thin white hand compassionately on Rougon's broad back*) "There, there, my son! It is the will of God."

ROUGON. (*Startled by the sound of a voice, jumps up from his chair*) "Eh?" (*Stares at the priest with dazed eyes*)

THE PRIEST. (*With a sad smile*) "Oh, come now, it isn't possible that you've forgotten me."

ROUGON. (*Snatching off his cap respectfully*) "Pardon, Father. I was - I didn't know - you see - all this - "

THE PRIEST. (*Gently*) "I have heard of your loss. I understand."

ROUGON. "But take the chair, Father." (*Bitterly*) "I am lucky to have it left to offer you."

THE PRIEST. (*Sitting down*) "You must not brood over your misfortunes. Many, a great many, have suffered even more than you. You must learn to bear these burdens as they come, at such a dreadful time as this, and pray to God for strength. We must all bow ourselves before His will."

ROUGON. "His will? Ha! No, the good God would not punish me so, - I, who have harmed no one." (*Furiously*) "It is all these cursed Pruss - "

THE PRIEST. "Ssshh!" (*After a pause*) "Such thoughts may rest in the heart, but to let them rise to the lips is hardly wise - now."

ROUGON. "What matter if they should hear? I am finished, me! They can do no more but kill me." (*He sits on the edge of the table. A heavy sob shakes his bowed shoulders.*)

THE PRIEST. (*After a pause during which he gazes sadly at the face of the dead young soldier*) "You must not mourn his loss so bitterly. He has given his life for his country. He is at rest with God. You should feel proud of him."

ROUGON. (*Dully*) "Yes, he is - at rest - in heaven. And, look you, Father, you remember, this was the day - today he was to have been married."

THE PRIEST. (*In accents of deep grief*) "True, true, I had forgotten. Poor boy, poor boy - and poor Louise!"

ROUGON. "And my poor old woman - Ah, good God, what have we done? All this - in one day!"

THE PRIEST. "Your wife - she doesn't know?"

ROUGON. "No. This morning, look you, I sent her away. It was Charles who came to me this morning - in his new uniform

- he who lies there so still now - he whom they have murdered, those cursed Prussians!"

THE PRIEST. "Ssshh! Would you bring more misfortune upon yourself?"

ROUGON. (*Springing to his feet in a frenzy*) "Ah, how I would love to slaughter them, to grind my heel in their fat faces, to, - to - "

THE PRIEST. "Calm yourself, for the love of heaven, my good Rougon! Will it improve matters, think you, to have you, too, shot? Do not forget your poor old wife. You must be careful for her sake, if for nothing else."

ROUGON. (*Sullenly slouching back to his seat on the table*) "It is hard, name of a dog, it is hard. I feel like a coward, me, to stand by and do nothing."

THE PRIEST. (*In low tones*) "Be comforted. The hour of retribution will yet strike. The end is not yet. Your son Charles will be avenged."

ROUGON. (*Shaking his head doubtfully*) "There are so many."

THE PRIEST. "But you were telling me about your wife. You sent her away this morning?"

ROUGON. "If the good God so pleases she is in Brussels by now. For, look you, Charles came to me this morning. 'My father' he said, 'I am afraid there will be fighting here today. I have warned the family of Louise and she is to flee with them to Brussels. I have arranged that Mother should go with them; and you, too, my father.' 'But no,' I said, 'It is right for your mother. She shall go. As you say, it will be no place for women if there be fighting. But me, no, I shall stay.' 'Mind you, then, Father, no shooting!' Charles said as he kissed me good-bye and ran to join the regiment on the village place, 'or they will shoot you like a dog'."

THE PRIEST. "You see! Your son gave you the best advice. Remember you are not a soldier."

ROUGON. (*Proudly*) "If I were not too old I should have been in a uniform this long time gone. Too old! The fools! As if I could not shoot straighter than all these boys!"

THE PRIEST. "There are other things to consider, my poor Rougon. Someone must gather in the harvest if we are not all to starve."

ROUGON. (*Fiercely*) "The harvest? What is there left? First it is the French who take away my two fine horses that I have saved up every centime two years to buy - and leave me a scrap of paper; then - "

THE PRIEST. "The French are our friends; in due time you shall be paid."

ROUGON. "Bah, promises!"

THE PRIEST. (*Earnestly*) "At a time like this all must bear their share of sacrifice."

ROUGON. "All who wanted war, yes; but we who desired nothing more than to be left in peace to till our fields? Look you, my Father, why should we be robbed and plundered and our homes blown apart by their accursed cannon?"

THE PRIEST. (*Shaking his head, sadly*) "God knows. Our poor country is a lamb among wolves."

ROUGON. (*Raising his voice excitedly*) "The first shell that burst in our village - do you know where it struck?"

THE PRIEST. "No."

ROUGON. "Out there - on my barn - setting it in flames - killing my two cows one of which I was to have given Charles, with half of my farm, as a wedding present - burning up all my hay I had gathered for the winter." (*Stamping his foot in his rage*) "Ah, those dirty beasts!"

THE PRIEST. "Ssshh! They are all around."

ROUGON. "And then, look you, the cavalry ride over my fields trampling my grain beneath their horses, the artillery wheels tear up the earth, the cannon blow my home to pieces - as you see." (*Bitterly*) "Harvest? There is nothing left to harvest but dirt and stones!"

THE PRIEST. (*To change the subject which is rapidly infuriating the old man*) "You may well give thanks to the good God that your wife is safe in Brussels."

ROUGON. "They started early this morning, as I have said, and the family of Louise has relatives in Brussels. She is safe, God be thanked." (*With a grief-stricken glance at the body of his son*) "But when she knows - and Louise who also loved him so - Oh, my God!" (*He chokes back a sob.*)

THE PRIEST. "God give them strength to bear it."

ROUGON. (*Indicating his son*) "He wanted me to go with them. He was afraid I would do something rash if I stayed. But I have been calm. But, name of a dog, it has been hard - when I saw them trampling my wheat - those pigs - when I saw the ashes which had been my barn - and this house, as you see, where I had lived so many years - this finger itched to press the trigger and send at least one to hell for payment."

THE PRIEST. "My son, my son!"

ROUGON. "Your pardon, my Father. Had it not been for the promise I had given Charles, I would have taken the old rifle from where I have it hidden in there" (*He indicates with a nod of his head the room on the left*) "and - "

THE PRIEST. (*Casting an apprehensive glance toward the street*) "Ssshh! Be careful what you say in so loud a tone. Their soldiers are everywhere. But where were you when all this fighting was taking place?"

ROUGON. "I was hiding in the well. I had placed a board across, on which I could stand and see what took place through the chinks in the stones. I wanted to see - him."

THE PRIEST. "See - Charles? How could - "

ROUGON. "His part of the regiment was behind the wall in the orchard not one hundred meters away. I could watch him clearly."

THE PRIEST. (*To himself, half-aloud*) "Poor man!"

ROUGON. "At first it was all right. Their infantry came up so close to each other that not even a child could have missed them. Bang! and they were toppled over before they had even reached the foot of the hill. I laughed. I thought it was all finished. I could see Charles laughing and talking with his comrades - and then - " (*He stops, shaking his head despondently*)

THE PRIEST. "And then?"

ROUGON. "One of their devilish flying machines which look like the great birds flew overhead, far-up. All shot at it but it was too far away. It flew back to them, and a minute later, look you, I saw white puffs of smoke on all the hills over to the west; then bang! crash! I could not hear; my ears were cracked with the din. There was dust, and falling walls, and by barn blazing. Ah, those accursed cannon? I climbed out of the well and ran to the barn."

THE PRIEST. "In the midst of all those bursting shells?"

ROUGON. "I trembled with rage. I had no fear of their cannon. I remembered only the cow, the pretty little cow, I was to give to Charles. But I could do nothing. Not all the fire-engines in Belgium could have saved it. I ran back to the well. Ssszzz! went the bullets all round. As I was climbing over I was stunned by a terrible crash. The roof of this house tumbled in - as you see."

THE PRIEST. "And you remained in the well all during the battle?"

ROUGON. "Yes - until I saw Charles fall. He was just aiming his rifle over the wall when I saw him throw up his hands, spin around like a top, and fall on his face. I ran down and carried him back on my shoulders to the well - but it was too late. He was dead." (*He stops abruptly, choking back a sob.*)

THE PRIEST. (*After a pause*) "Requiescat in pace. His life was ever a happy one. He never knew the cares and worries that come with the years and the ceaseless struggle for bread. He loved and was loved. He died the death of the brave." (*Gently*) "Is it not better after all - as it is?" (*Rougon does not answer.*) "Can you not console yourself with that thought?"

ROUGON. "Perhaps. Who knows? But, look you, it is hard for me - and for Louise - and most of all for his mother whose baby he was."

THE PRIEST. "You all loved him, did everything in your power to make him happy. You have nothing with which to reproach yourselves."

ROUGON. "But now - what shall I do? Look you, it was for him we worked and saved, his mother and I; that he might never have to know, as we had known, what it is to be poor and hungry." (*Despondently*) "And now - we are old - what use to work? There is nothing left but death."

THE PRIEST. "You have each other"

ROUGON. "Yes, we have each other. Were it not for the thought of my poor Margot I had let these butchers kill me before this."

THE PRIEST. (*Sternly*) "I do not like to hear you talk in that manner. You must realize well, that in its time of stress, your country has need of you; as much need of you as of her soldiers. You must not be rash. You must live and help and bear your part of her burden as best you can. It is your duty."

ROUGON. "Yes, yes, I well know it; but - "

THE PRIEST. "Above all, you have to exercise control over your hasty temper. You must realize that you will best serve your country and revenge your personal wrongs by living and helping, not by willfully seeking death. You must remember you are a civilian and, according to the rules of war, you have no right to fight. Your part lies elsewhere. Let others shoot the guns."

ROUGON. (*Disgustedly*) "Bah! The children they have as soldiers cannot shoot. With my little rifle in there I could pick off more Prussian swine than a whole regiment of youngsters like my poor Charles." (*Scornfully*) "Yet they tell me I am too old to enlist! Dolts!"

THE PRIEST. (*Rising and laying his hand on Rougon's back - with solemn earnestness*) "My son, before I leave, I want you to swear to me before the God who watches over us, that you will remember what I have said and not allow your temper to force you to violence."

ROUGON. (*Sullenly*) "I promise. I swear it."

THE PRIEST. (*Patting him on the back*) "There, now you are sensible, more like yourself." (*He stands looking down at Charles*) "I would advise you as to the burial of Charles." (*Rougon groans*) "Let it be done as secretly as possible. Let us avoid all provocation, and on their heads be it if misfortune happens. Perhaps tonight would be best."

ROUGON. "Ah, no, no, no! Please, my Father, not yet! To-night let him remain here in his home, the house he was born in, with me."

THE PRIEST. "So be it. Tomorrow night, then. You will let me know what time you wish it to be."

ROUGON. "Very well, my Father."

THE PRIEST. "And now I must go; but first let us kneel down and humbly offer up a prayer for the repose of his soul." (*They kneel down beside the dead body. The priest commences to intone a prayer in which the words "Almighty God," "Merciful," "Infinite justice," "Infinite love," "Infinite pity," "Thy son Jesus," "We, Thy children," "Praise Thy infinite goodness," stand out from the general mumble of sing-song sentences. Perhaps a sense of the crushing irony of this futile prayer penetrates the sorrow-numbed brain of Rougon and proves the last straw which breaks down his self-control; for he interrupts the droning supplications of the priest with a groan of agony, throws himself beside the young soldier's body, and sobs brokenly:* "Charles, Charles, my little one! Oh, why did not God take me instead!"*

THE PRIEST. (*After a pause - wiping the tears from his eyes with his large handkerchief*) "Come, come, it is hard, I know, but you must bear it like a man. God's will be done! He, too, had a Son who died for others. Pray to Him and He will comfort you in your affliction."

ROUGON. (*Placing his hand gently on his son's face*) "Cold! Cold! He who was so alive and smiling only this morning." (*A step is heard on the road outside. The two get hastily to their feet as a young man in the grey uniform of a German captain of infantry appears at one of the gaps of the wall.*)

THE CAPTAIN. (*Entering and turning to the priest*) "Are you the - " (*Seeing the body on the floor*) "I beg your pardon."

THE PRIEST. (*Coldly*) "What is your wish?"

THE CAPTAIN. (*Twirling his blond mustache fiercely to hide his embarrassment*) "Again, I ask pardon. I meant no disrespect." (*Taking off his helmet impressively - He is a very young captain*) "I honor the brave dead on whichever side they fall."

THE PRIEST. (*Indicating Rougon who has slunk off to the other side of the table and is controlling his hatred and rage with very apparent effort*) "It is his son."

THE CAPTAIN. "Ah! Too bad! The fortunes of war. Today, him; tomorrow, me, perhaps. Are you the curé of the village."

THE PRIEST. "I am."

THE CAPTAIN. "I have been seeking you ever since we occupied the place."

THE PRIEST. "I returned but a short time ago from Brussels where I had been called to make my report to the Bishop. I knew nothing of the fighting here or I should have returned sooner." (*Sadly*) "There were many, perhaps, who died needing me. But what is it you wish?"

THE CAPTAIN. "I was sent by the colonel to find you and deliver his orders. There seems to be no one of civil authority left in the village - else I should not intrude upon you."

THE PRIEST. "I am listening."

THE CAPTAIN. (*Oratorically*) "It is the colonel's wish that you warn the inhabitants against committing any violence against our soldiers. Civilians caught with arms will be immediately shot." (*The Priest casts a significant glance at Rougon who scowls and mutters to himself.*) "Is that clear?"

THE PRIEST. "Quite."

THE CAPTAIN. "On the other hand all we demand of you will be paid for in cash. Let all your parishioners return to their work without fear of molestation. We make no war upon the helpless." (*With complacent pride*) "I hope I make my meaning clear. I flatter myself my French is not so bad."

THE PRIEST. (*With cold politeness*) "You speak it very well, Monsieur. You may tell your colonel that I will do all in my power to impress his words upon the minds of my people - not that I respect his orders or admit his right to give them to a man of peace, but because I have the welfare of my people at heart."

THE CAPTAIN. "Good. I will tell him. And now I will say 'au revoir' for I, too, have my duties to perform. We march from here immediately."

THE PRIEST. (*Significantly*) "Adieu." (*The Captain goes out.*)

ROUGON. (*Raging*) "Dog of a Prussian!"

THE PRIEST. "Silence! Are you a fool?" (*While he is speaking an awkward peasant boy of about fifteen with a broad face appears at the breech in the rear wall. His clothes are mud-stained and ragged and he is trembling with fear. He breathes in great shuddering gasps. There is a cut on his forehead beneath which the blood has dried in reddish-brown streaks.*)

ROUGON. (*Hears the noise*) "What's that?" (*They both turn around and see the boy.*)

THE PRIEST. "Why, it's Jean! Whatever are you doing skulking around like that?"

JEAN. (*Stopping uneasily as if he intended to run away again*) "Nothing, nothing."

THE PRIEST. "Come over here." (*Jean does not move but stares at him with frightened eyes.*) "Don't you hear me speaking to you? What is the matter with you?"

JEAN. (*Faintly*) "I am afraid."

THE PRIEST. "Of me? Come, this is ridiculous."

JEAN. (*His lips trembling*) "I am afraid - of them. Everything - blows up."

ROUGON. "Come to the good father when he speaks to you, stupid dolt! Or I shall find a good strong stick and - "

THE PRIEST "Hush, you are only frightening him. Come to me, Jean, like a good boy." (*Jean goes slowly to the priest who puts an arm about his shoulders*) "Why, you're trembling like a leaf! Did the battle frighten you?"

JEAN. "No, no, no! I don't know."

ROUGON. (*Contemptuously*) "The battle? He was never near the fighting. It was bad enough for we others without having this half-witted calf around. So we sent him away with the women this morning." (*To Jean*) "Answer me, you, how is it you are back here?"

JEAN. (*Trembling*) "I don't know.

ROUGON. (*Roughly*) "Name of a dog, what do you know? Did we send you away with the women this morning or didn't we?"

JEAN. (*Uncertainly*) "Yes - went away - this morning."

THE PRIEST. "Hush, Rougon, you are only frightening the poor fellow. Jean, listen to me and stop trembling. I shall not let anyone hurt you. I have always been your good friend, have I not?"

JEAN. "Yes - you are my friend."

THE PRIEST. "Of course I am; and while I am around there is nothing you need fear. Come now, tell me like a good lad; you went away with the others this morning, didn't you?"

JEAN. "Yes, Father."

THE PRIEST. "Then how do you happen to be here now? Why did you return to the village? Your clothes are in a shocking state. Where have you been hiding and how did you get that cut on your forehead?"

JEAN. (*Feeling the cut on his forehead with a dazed air*) "It hurts."

THE PRIEST. "You will come home with me presently and we will wash that nasty cut and wrap it up in a nice clean bandage. Then you may be sure you will no longer feel any hurt at all. But first tell me - '''

JEAN. "I don't know. I ran and ran - and I came here."

THE PRIEST. "But something must have happened to make you run. Come, tell us, what was it?"

JEAN. (*Vaguely*) "We left here and walked a long, long ways. Some rode in wagons but I was walking."

ROUGON. "And did you see Mother Rougon there, and Louise?"

JEAN. (*In a strange tone - with a shudder*) "Yes, I saw them, I saw them." (*Rougon gives a grunt of satisfaction.*)

THE PRIEST. "Go on, my son, tell us what happened next."

JEAN. "We could hear shots. We hurried faster. The horses galloped. The women commenced to scream and cry. Always the firing was louder. We didn't see any soldiers for a long time. Then we came upon lots of bodies - men from our army and others dressed in grey."

ROUGON. (*In growing alarm*) "Name of a dog, why didn't you turn back, eh?"

JEAN. (*Vaguely*) I don't know." (*He drones on in his expressionless voice*) "The women were praying. They were afraid. They wanted us to hurry up and get to Brussels. We beat the horses. The hills were covered with white spots like, - like daisies; and they floated 'way up in the air." (*He makes a queer awkward gesture upward.*)

ROUGON. "Idiot! What is all this foolish talk?"

THE PRIEST. (*Gently*) "It was the smoke from the guns you saw, my child."

JEAN. (*Very slowly - trying his best to imitate the exact sound*) "Boom! Boom! Boom! I couldn't hear what anyone was saying." (*He pauses.*)

ROUGON. "Why do you stop, stupid? Go on, go on, or - " (*He shakes his clenched fist at the boy.*)

THE PRIEST. "Silence, Rougon! Give the poor lad a chance."

JEAN. (*In flat, monotonous tones*) "Something blew up in a field by the road and threw dirt and stones on us. The horses were afraid. They ran faster. Then we came to the top of a hill. Lots of the soldiers in our army were there hiding in a long ditch. They shouted for us to run away. Then - then - then - "

THE PRIEST. (*Anxiously*) "Yes? (*Rougon stands tensely with averted face as if afraid to listen.*)

JEAN. (*Throwing both his arms into the air with a wild gesture*) "Then everything around blew up." (*In flat tones*) "Something hit me on the head. I laid down for a while. When I got up I couldn't see any of the rest. There were bodies all around. I saw Mother Rougon - "

THE PRIEST. (*Clinging to a last shred of hope*) "Alive and unharmed?" (*But Rougon has guessed the worst and stands as if in a stupor, clenching and unclenching his big red hands, his features working convulsively.*)

JEAN. "She was lying on the ground. She had a big hole here" (*Pointing to his chest*) "and blood all over - bright and red like - like flowers."

ROUGON. (*Dully*) "Dead! She, too!"

JEAN. "And Louise had a hole in her head, here" (*Pointing to his forehead*) "and - "

THE PRIEST. (*Distracted with horror*) "Enough! Stop! We have heard all we care to, do you hear?"

JEAN. "So I ran, and ran, and ran, and ran, and ran." (*His words die away into a murmur - He stares straight before him like one in a trance.*)

THE PRIEST. "Merciful God, have pity!"

ROUGON. (*Slowly - as if the meaning of Jean's words were just commencing to dawn on him*) "So - they are gone, too - the old woman - and Louise - " (*Licks his lips with his dry tongue*) "Everything is gone."

(*There is a long silence. The priest dabs with his big hand-kerchief at the tears which are welling into his eyes. Jean wanders over to the breach in the wall and stands looking down the road. A loud bugle call is heard. Jean darts back into the room.*)

JEAN. (*Waving his arms, cries in terrified tones*) "They are coming. They are coming this way!" (*He runs to the right corner of the room and crouches there trembling, seeking to hide himself in the fallen ruins.*)

ROUGON. "So - *they* are coming?" (*He strides resolutely across the room and enters the room on left.*)

THE PRIEST. (*Alarmed by the expression on Rougon's face*) "Rougon! Rougon! What are you going to do?" (*He receives no answer. A moment later Rougon re-enters the room carrying a long-barrelled rifle.*)

THE PRIEST. (*Seizing him by the arm*) "No, no, I beseech you!"

ROUGON. (*Roughly throwing the priest aside*) "Let me alone!" (*He half-kneels beside one of the breeches in the wall - then speaks in a voice of deadly calmness.*) "They will not pass here. They are going to turn off at the fork in the road. It is near enough, however." (*The rhythmic tramp of the marching troops can be faintly heard.*)

THE PRIEST. (*In agony*) "In the name of God I implore you - "

ROUGON. "Bah, God!" (*He takes careful aim and fires*) "That for Margot!" (*Loads and fires again.*) "That for Louise!" (*Cries of rage and running footsteps are heard. Rougon is reloading his rifle when the Captain and four German privates rush in. Rougon struggles but is disarmed and forced back to the wall on left. He stands proudly, calmly awaiting his fate. One of the soldiers siezes the priest.*)

THE SOLDIER. (*To the Captain*) "Was mit dem Priester?"

ROUGON. (*To the Captain*) "The good father did nothing. He but did his best to hold my arm and stop me. It is I alone who did the shooting, Dog of a Prussian!"

THE CAPTAIN. "Is this true, priest?"

THE PRIEST. "It is as he tells you. I tried to restrain him - not for your sakes, but for his own."

THE CAPTAIN. (*To the soldier*) "Las den Priester gehen!" (*The soldier releases the priest. The Captain turns to Rougon.*) "If you have a prayer to say, be quick!" (*The four soldiers line up in front of Rougon and face him across the body of Charles.*)

ROUGON. (*With angry scorn*) "I want no prayers!"

THE PRIEST. "Rougon!"

ROUGON. (*Furiously*) "To hell with your prayers!"

THE PRIEST. (*Supplicatingly*) "Make your peace with God, my son!"

ROUGON. (*Spitting on the floor, fiercely*) "That for your God who allows such things to happen!" (*To the Captain*) "I am ready, pig!"

THE CAPTAIN. (*To the soldiers*) "Gewehr! Heraus!" (*The soldiers take aim.*)

THE PRIEST. "May God have mercy on - "

THE CAPTAIN. "Feuer!" (*A crashing report. Rougon pitches forward on his face, quivers for a moment, is still. The soldiers file out to the road. The Captain turns to the horrified priest.*)

THE CAPTAIN. (*Shrugging his shoulders*) "It is the law." (*He follows the soldiers.*)

THE PRIEST. (*Looking down with infinite compassion at the still bodies of father and son.*) "Alas, the laws of men!" (*The sun has set. The twilight is fading grayly into night. From the heap of wreckage in the right corner comes the sound of stifled weeping.*)

THE CURTAIN FALLS

"SERVITUDE" (1914)

A Play In Three Acts

Characters

DAVID ROYLSTON, *Playwright and novelist.*

ALICE ROYLSTON, *his wife.*

DAVIE ⎱
RUTH ⎰ *their children.*

GEORGE FRAZER, *a broker.*

ETHEL FRAZER, *his wife.*

BENTON, *a man-servant.*

WESON, *a gardener.*

ACT I

ACT I. David Roylston's study in his house at Tarryville-on-Hudson, N. Y. - about ten o'clock in the evening.

TIME: The present day.

SCENE: *The study in the house of David Roylston at Tarry-ville-on-Hudson, New York. In the middle of the far side of the room, a fireplace. To the right of it, a door. The remaining space of the back wall is covered by book-cases which frame the fireplace and door. In the left foreground, another door. Next to it, a writing desk. Still farther back, a book-case. On the right, a leather sofa and armchairs. On either side of the sofa, an open window looking out on the garden. In the center of the room, a table on which are a heap of books and an electric reading lamp with a green shade. A few framed prints of Old Masters are hung on the walls.*

It is about ten o'clock on a sultry night in early May.

David Roylston is seated at the table, writing. He is a tall, slender, dark-haired man of thirty-five with large handsome features, a strong, ironical mouth half-hidden by a black mustache, and keenly-intelligent dark eyes. He has taken off his coat which hangs from the back of his chair. He wears a white shirt with soft collar and black bow tie, grey trousers, and low tan shoes with rubber soles.

Benton enters from the door at the rear and stands waiting for Roylston to notice his presence. He is fifty-five, clean-shaven, discreetly soft-spoken. One of his eyes is badly crossed giving him a look of sly villainy quite out of keeping with his placid temperament. He wears a livery.

ROYLSTON. (*looking up from his writing*) "Well, Benton?"

BENTON. "Shall I shut the windows, sir? It's started to rain a little."

ROYLSTON. "No, I will close them myself when I go to bed."

BENTON. (*reproachfully*) "They were open when I came down this morning, sir."

ROYLSTON. "Were they? I must have forgotten all about

them last light. Never mind; there's nothing much worth the stealing in this house except ideas and the thieves of ideas are not usually housebreakers. But if it will ease your anxiety, you may close them. There's a draft in here.''

BENTON. "Yes, sir." (*He closes the windows.*)

ROYLSTON. "Any telephone calls while I was out?"

BENTON. "Mrs. Roylston called up, sir; wished me to tell you that she and the children had arrived safely in New York; had a very pleasant trip in the motor; roads were fine all the way down. She said the children were very excited to think they were really going to the theatre.''

ROYLSTON. (*abstractedly*) "Ah, indeed. No one else called up?''

BENTON. "No, sir."

ROYLSTON. "Not even the young lady who has" (*ironically*) "asked my advice so frequently of late?"

BENTON. "No, sir."

ROYLSTON. "Well, whenever the young lady in question calls up again you are to tell her I am writing and cannot be disturbed.''

BENTON. "Yes, sir."

ROYLSTON. (*impatiently*) "She is becoming a bore; and I am in the midst of a play and have no time for such foolishness.''

BENTON. "Very good, sir. Anything else before I go to bed, sir?''

ROYLSTON. "No, you may go." (*Benton takes Roylston's light overcoat, hat, and stick, which are lying on one of the armchairs, and starts to go out.*) "Leave those here. I may take a walk later on to get a breath of the Spring and blow the cobwebs out of my brain, and I don't care to be barking my shins in the dark hall." (*Benton lays them down again. A doorbell is heard ringing somewhere in the house.*) "Who can that be at this time of the night?" (*As Benton hurries out through the door on the left.*) "Remember, Benton, I'm busy - too busy to be disturbed."

BENTON. "Yes, sir." (*He goes out. Roylston bites his pen nervously, trying to concentrate his thoughts. A minute or so later Benton enters. He is visibly embarrassed and is turning over a card in his fingers.*)

ROYLSTON. "Well?"

BENTON. "It's a lady, sir."

ROYLSTON. "Has she gone?"

BENTON. "No, sir, she - "

ROYLSTON. (*frowning*) "Did you tell her I was busy?"

BENTON. "Yes, sir, but she said she must see you on a very important matter; said she wouldn't leave till she saw you. This is her card, sir."

ROYLSTON. (*looking at it*) "Mrs. George Frazer - hm - Mrs., eh?; never heard of her. An old crank of some kind, I suppose?"

BENTON. "Quite the other way, sir; young and pretty, I should say, if I'm any judge."

ROYLSTON. "Anyone come with her?"

BENTON. "I don't think so, sir"

ROYLSTON. "Alone, at this time of night, and" (*sarcastically*) "A lady, you say?"

BENTON. (*promptly*) "No doubt of that, sir; but dressed shabby almost, as if she'd seen better days; you know what I mean, sir."

ROYLSTON. (*cynically*) "Ah, then, I had better get my checkbook ready."

BENTON. "Beg your pardon, sir, but she doesn't seem that kind either; not like one that'd beg, I mean. I couldn't make her out exactly."

ROYLSTON. "Perhaps she's another aspiring playwright who wants me to write her last act for her. At any rate you have aroused my curiosity; so show her in here." (*He takes his coat off the back of the chair and puts it on.*)

BENTON. "Very well, sir." (*He goes out through the door on the left. A moment later he shows in Mrs. Frazer. She is a tall, strikingly beautiful woman about twenty-eight years old. Her complexion is pale; her eyes large, expressive, dark; her hair black and wavy; her figure inclining a little toward voluptuousness. There are shadows in under her eyes and her face is drawn. Her manner is troubled, nervous, uncertain. She has on a plain black dress such as is worn by the poorer class of working women.*)

ROYLSTON. (*getting up and staring at her with open admiration*) "Ah!" (*turning to Benton*) "You may go, Benton. I shan't need you again. I will take Mrs. - er (*looking at the card*) Mrs. Frazer to the door myself."

BENTON. "Yes, sir." (*He goes out.*)

MRS. FRAZER. (*uncertainly*) "I hope you will pardon - "

ROYLSTON. (*indicating the armchairs on the left*) "Won't you sit down, Mrs. Frazer?" (*She sits down in the one nearest to him*) "And now, what can I do for you?"

MRS. FRAZER. "I know this intrusion of mine is unpardonable. You must be terribly busy, and I have forced myself on you, interrupted your work - "

ROYLSTON. "You must not feel conscience-stricken about that. I was only puzzling over a problem in construction. I am glad to have my mind taken off it for a time."

MRS. FRAZER. "But my coming here at this time of the night and alone?" (*forcing a smile*) "What can you think of such a breach of all the conventions!"

ROYLSTON. (*dryly*) "You are the very first to accuse me of conventionality. I see nothing strange in your coming here when you wanted to, when you were able to. I have lived long enough in this suburb to know the difficulties of getting here at the time one wishes."

MRS. FRAZER. (*looking at him for a moment with a questioning smile*) "Can't you remember ever having seen me before?"

ROYLSTON. "No, I must confess - "

MRS. FRAZER. "And yet you have met me. I can, at least, plead that much justification for this encroachment on your time."

ROYLSTON. (*trying to remember*) "It's no use. My brain is too full of marionettes to recall flesh-and-blood realities. I confess to my shame I will have to ask you where it was."

MRS. FRAZER. "Oh, I did not dream of your remembering. We only spoke about two words to each other, and it was at least a year ago. You remember the ball Mr. Coleman, the artist, gave at his studio?"

ROYLSTON. "So it was there? It would be too trite for me to say I knew I had seen you before; but I really did have that feeling when you came in. One doesn't forget a face like yours. So it was at Coleman's studio? He and I have been friends for years."

MRS. FRAZER. "He is a very dear friend of my - of mine, also."

ROYLSTON. "Do take off your hat now that we know who's who. To see you sitting there with your hat on gives me the uncomfortable impression that this is a lawyer's office and you are consulting your attorney - and I warn you I am far from being a *legal* adviser."

MRS. FRAZER. (*takes off her hat and puts it on the sofa; leans back in her chair*) "I knew it. That is why I came."

ROYLSTON. "For advice?"

MRS. FRAZER. "Advice which I must have or - "

ROYLSTON. "Or?"

MRS. FRAZER. "The crowning disillusion."

ROYLSTON. (*smiling*) "I hope it is not about me, the illusion."

MRS. FRAZER. (*emphatically*) "It is about you but it is not an illusion."

ROYLSTON. "Certainty goeth before disappointment."

MRS. FRAZER. "In this case it must not. I have borne so much already, - I could not bear it. I must have something firm to stand on."

ROYLSTON. "Then it is not a play you come to consult me about?" (*seeing her mystified expression*) "I beg your pardon, but you know there are so many playwrights-in-embryo who come to me for suggestions about their work - as if I could help them; as if it were not absolutely necessary for them to work out their own salvation! - and I thought when you mentioned advice - "

MRS. FRAZER. (*smiling*) "I see. No, I almost wish it were. I would like to be able to write a play even if it were only a very bad one. It would at least prove I was capable of creating something; I'm afraid even that is beyond my power."

ROYLSTON. (*perfunctorily*) "One never knows till one tries. The thing to do is to make a start; and then, if necessary, realize one's mistake smilingly."

MRS. FRAZER. "I intend to try sometime." (*apologetically*) "I'm wasting your time and I will come to the point at once; or rather I will have to go back quite a ways to give you a clear idea of my present situation." (*nervously*) "Won't you smoke or appear occupied with something? I won't feel such an intruder if you do."

ROYLSTON. (*laughing*) "I would have done so before if I had known you didn't object."

MRS. FRAZER. "On the contrary, I like it. My hus - I have always been accustomed to men who smoked. My father was a great smoker."

ROYLSTON. (*who has taken a box of cigarettes from his pocket and lighted one*) "There." (*He leans back in his chair in an attitude of attention.*)

MRS. FRAZER. "To begin at the beginning; My father was a prominent lawyer with a wide practice. He died five years ago leaving a large estate to my mother who is still alive but in very feeble health. They had only two children, my brother. five years older than I am, and myself. I tell you all this because you lay such stress in all your books and plays on the influence of environment, and I want you to understand thoroughly what mine was. Being the baby and pet of the family you can readily guess how I was brought up - governesses, private tutors, and finally a finishing school. Of course at the end of their elaborate system of education I knew only what a young lady of my position should know - nothing of any value."

ROYLSTON. (*smiling*) "Naturally; but you have progressed wonderfully since then."

MRS. FRAZER. "If I have, I have paid for it; and whatever progress I have made I owe to you."

ROYLSTON. (*wonderingly*) "To me?"

MRS. FRAZER. "We haven't come to that part of the story yet. When I returned home from the finishing school my life became one long round of receptions, parties, balls, and so forth, until, in spite of the fact that at that time I was only interested in the most superficial things, I became surfeited, bored, and felt a longing to break away and experience something of more interest."

ROYLSTON. "You wished to try your wings."

MRS. FRAZER. "Yes, that was it. It was about this time I met Mr. Frazer, the man who afterward became my husband. He was then, and still is, a broker on the New York Stock Exchange. He fascinated me. I seemed to see personified in him all I had read about the" (*sarcastically*) "financial giants, the daring gamblers who fought their battles to the bitter end of ruin. The house he was connected with is one of the largest on the Exchange and some of the so-called Napoleons of finance, whose names were forever in newspaper headlines, did their business through it. I thought of him doing his part in their gigantic enterprises, laboring to effect ever larger combinations in order that this glorious country might thrive and become ever greater and more productive." (*with a short laugh*) "You can see what a child I was; but I'm afraid you're not listening."

ROYLSTON. (*eagerly*) "I assure you you are mistaken. I am intensely interested. I was simply trying to recall something. Do you know when I watch you and listen to you talk I am forcibly reminded of some other woman. The likeness is so perfect it's uncanny."

MRS. FRAZER. "May I ask who it is?"

ROYLSTON. "That's exactly what I cannot recollect. I am

sure it's someone I know intimately and yet, for the life of me, I cannot bring the exact person to my mind."

MRS. FRAZER. "How strange."

ROYLSTON. "But I'm interrupting you. Please go on with your story."

MRS. FRAZER. "Well, the inevitable happened. I fell in love with George - Mr. Frazer - and he with me, and after a short engagement we were married. My family approved of him in every way. I believe they cherished the same illusion about his business, in a modified form, perhaps, as I did."

ROYLSTON. "Do you not think your husband also had the same illusions?"

MRS. FRAZER. "It would be hard to say. In justice to him I must acknowledge he always seemed to idealize it. He never could see his business in all its hideousness as I came to see it, and I don't think he wore a mask just for my benefit; but you never can tell."

ROYLSTON. "Most of them can't see the unpleasant side. It becomes so much a part of themselves, you know. And after you were married?"

MRS. FRAZER. "Oh, the usual honeymoon trip to Europe with it's inevitable visits to Westminster Abbey, the tomb of Napoleon, the Cologne Cathedral, and other points of interest."

ROYLSTON. (*ironically*) "How ideal!"

MRS. FRAZER. "And yet I was very happy, or thought I was happy, which is much the same thing. Of course in the light of what I now know, of what you have taught me, I can see it was merely a stupid happiness, the content of the born blind who have never seen the light."

ROYLSTON. "And I am to blame for your enlightenment?"

MRS. FRAZER. "To blame?"

ROYLSTON. "Since it has made you unhappy it must be blameworthy."

MRS. FRAZER. (*with fine scorn*) "What is such sluggish content worth? When you had opened my eyes to the truth I repudiated it. I felt I must win to a higher plane - or remain unhappy."

ROYLSTON. (*bewildered - running his fingers through his hair - with laughing impatience*) "How you do remind me of someone! And yet I cannot remember - But tell me how this great change came about. After your return from your honeymoon I suppose your husband laid aside his role of lover and became the business man once more, leaving you to ornament his home, and brood, and read my novels and plays."

MRS. FRAZER. "That is what you would naturally think, isn't it? However, you are quite wrong. My husband was as much the lover on the day I left him as he had been when we were married seven years before."

ROYLSTON. "Then you have left him?"

MRS. FRAZER. "Yes, eight months ago."

ROYLSTON. "Have you no children?"

MRS. FRAZER. "No. I used to be very sorry we had not; but now I am glad. It would have made it so much harder for me when the time came to free myself."

ROYLSTON. "You fell in love with someone else?"

MRS. FRAZER. (*flushing*) "If I had ceased to love my husband it is no reason why - "

ROYLSTON. (*smiling*) "You must not be offended. It usually happens that way you know."

MRS. FRAZER. (*earnestly*) "I was in love with an ideal -

the ideal of self-realization, of the duty of the individual to assert its supremacy and demand the freedom necessary for its development. You had taught me that ideal and it was that which came in conflict with my marriage. I saw I could never hope to grow in the stifling environment of married life - so I broke away."

ROYLSTON. (*gravely*) "Please tell me in what manner I effected this change in you."

MRS. FRAZER. "I bought one of your novels one day about two years ago, more out of curiosity than anything else. It was the one about Wall Street."

ROYLSTON. "You mean 'The Street'."

MRS. FRAZER. "Yes, that's the one."

ROYLSTON. "Then it was that book of mine which disillusioned you about your husband's business?"

MRS. FRAZER. "Yes. When I first read it I couldn't believe it. I began to ask George questions about his deals and so forth. He was surprised and happy to find me interested in his work and he finally used to explain all his transactions to me - and then I knew."

ROYLSTON. "Hm."

MRS. FRAZER. "I tried to persuade him to go into something else. He acknowledged there was a lot of truth in your book but said there were two ways of looking at everything. When I pleaded with him he laughed and called me his 'dear little muckraker'."

ROYLSTON. (*smiling*) "So you became disillusioned about the broker - but how about the man?"

MRS. FRAZER. "Your book made me long to read what you had to say about other things. I bought all your published works, and went to see all your plays, not once but many times.

It dawned upon me gradually that the life he and I were living together was the merest sham; that we were contented because he was too busy and I was too lazy to analyze our position, to stop and think. For a long time I was very unhappy. I knew what I must do but I did not have the courage to do it."

ROYLSTON. (*impatiently*) "Why didn't you tell him frankly how you felt?"

MRS. FRAZER. "I couldn't. You see he was so good and kind to me and it seemed such heartless cruelty to hurt him. All the time I felt myself being ground smaller and smaller day by day. I discovered that he and I had not a thought in common. Everything he was interested in was so shallow. He never concerned himself with what lay beneath the surface and I know my thoughts bored him although he was far too kind to ever show it. He observed the change in me and it worried him but the only remedies he could suggest were" (*with a short laugh*) "Southern California, a trip to Europe, or some other change of air. When I refused to go away he was at a loss what to do. I think toward the end he suspected I was in love with someone else."

ROYLSTON. (*with a cynical smile*) "I'll wager he did."

MRS. FRAZER. "I resolved not to think. I plunged into all sorts of activities to try and forget myself. I learned shorthand and typewriting - "

ROYLSTON. (*interrupting her enthusiastically*) "Good! That is your salvation."

MRS. FRAZER. (*wearily*) "My soul refused to be lulled to sleep and there came a day when I left a note for my husband and left the house. I had been to see your play 'Sacrifice' the night before for the tenth time. It seemed to breathe a message to me over the footlights. You remember when Mrs.

Harding in the play leaves her husband with the words: 'I have awakened!'?''

ROYLSTON. (*his eyes searching hers with keen questioning*) ''Yes, but Mrs. Harding has a lover to go to.''

MRS. FRAZER. (*bearing his scrutiny unflinchingly*) ''And I have an ideal which I love. When I heard her say those words that night they impressed me as never before. I felt that I, too, had awakened; that the time had come to assert my - ''

ROYLSTON. (*with a sudden exclamation - interrupting her*) ''The puzzle is solved. What a dolt I am! It is Mrs. Harding in my play you resemble so much.''

MRS. FRAZER. (*surprised*) ''Oh, is it? I saw the play so many times, you see.''

ROYLSTON. ''And you left your husband the next day?''

MRS. FRAZER. ''Yes. I sold some things which I had a right to call my own and bought a plain black dress. I knew I would have to become a worker, a wage-earner, and I wished to take nothing with me to remind me of the old life.''

ROYLSTON. (*sympathetically*) ''I can imagine the ordeals you have been through since then. When one is beautiful it is doubly hard.''

MRS. FRAZER. (*blushing - hurriedly*) ''At first I missed all the little comforts and luxuries I had been used to. I never knew till I had to do without them how they had grown into my life. I got bravely over that. I found it very hard to get work and harder still to keep it. The men were all such beasts and the women I had to come in contact with were so unintelligent and ordinary.''

ROYLSTON. (*dryly*) ''You'll find most people are - rather ordinary.''

MRS. FRAZER. "In my last position I really thought for a time my employer was a gentleman. I discovered he was only playing a part to throw me off my guard and he turned out the worst of all. And then the unspeakably long nights in the dingy hall bedroom of a boarding house with no one to speak to, no money, no place to go; not able even to take a walk alone on the streets for fear of the insults, the smirking groups in the doorways and on the corners. Oh, yes, it has been hard!" (*her voice trembling*) "It has been almost more than I could endure."

ROYLSTON. (*kindly*) "Come; it was your ordeal of fire and you have born up wonderfully. Have you never received word from your husband?"

MRS. FRAZER. "That is the worst of all. He has haunted me, waited for me at the doors of boarding houses, at the entrance of office buildings where I worked, pleading with me to come back, offering to do anything I wished, trying to force money on me, even pushing it in under the door of my room. He cannot understand what has come over me. I think he really believes I am the victim of a mad infatuation for a married man; and yet he has had me followed continually, to protect me, as he says, not to spy on me, and he knows I have seen no one." (*putting her hands over her face with a sob*) "And he looks so unhappy, so miserable. I feel so guilty whenever I see him."

ROYLSTON. (*gently*) "Are you sure you no longer love him?"

MRS. FRAZER. (*hysterically*) "Oh, love, love, what is love? How can I know? I am certain I could no longer live with him. How can you doubt it after all I have told you? I know that I like him very much and do not want to see him suffer on my account."

ROYLSTON. (*after a pause - frowning*) "Have you stopped

to think that you might have been followed here?"

MRS. FRAZER. "I am certain I was not. He has given up hope. I haven't seen him in over a month. Besides, I took special pains to throw anyone off the track. I went down to the office building where I used to work this morning and left by a side entrance. I used the freight elevator to come down in. No one could have seen me."

ROYLSTON. "Where have you been all day?"

MRS. FRAZER. "Sitting on a bench in Central Park."

ROYLSTON. "But good heavens, Mrs. Frazer, why didn't you come during the day?"

MRS. FRAZER. "I was afraid you might be out. You see, I had read in the paper that you always worked at night and I felt pretty sure of finding you. I could not afford more than one trip. To be quite frank with you, it was with the last dollar I had in the world that I came out here."

ROYLSTON. "But if I had not been at home?"

MRS. FRAZER. (firmly) "I should have waited until you came. No matter how, I should have waited."

ROYLSTON. (plainly embarrassed - getting up and walking nervously about the room) "You have been frank with me, Mrs. Frazer. Will you permit me to be the same?"

MRS. FRAZER. "I wish you to be so."

ROYLSTON. "You promise to take no offense at what I am going to ask you?"

MRS. FRAZER. "I am not afraid. I know you are trying to help me."

ROYLSTON. "I am glad of that. What I want to ask is: Will you let me help you in - er - a pecuniary way?"

MRS. FRAZER. (*rather indignantly*) "How could you think so?"

ROYLSTON. "I mean as a loan, you know. You really ought to - "

MRS. FRAZER. "You know I could not."

ROYLSTON. "Then you have not freed yourself from all prejudices after all. You will certainly let me see to it that you get a position where you will be well paid and respected?"

MRS. FRAZER. "Gladly, and be more than grateful for your assistance."

ROYLSTON. (*with a sigh of relief*) "Then, that is settled." (*Mrs. Frazer suddenly breaks down and commences to sob. Roylston goes to her and lays his hand on her shoulder.*) "There, there, Mrs. Frazer. I know it has been hard. It's bound to be, you know, for a woman in your position. The future will be much easier, you'll find. Please don't break down that way." (*a pause*) "I feel as if I were responsible for all this and yet - "

MRS. FRAZER. (*wiping her tears away and trying to control herself*) "You don't understand. You are only looking at the material side. I don't care about that. What I came here to demand - yes, demand, for I have a right to do so - was certainty, the assurance that I am on the right path. These past few weeks with their sleepless nights have been terrible."

ROYLSTON. "How can I - "

MRS. FRAZER. "Had I the right to do what I did? To cause others so much suffering? Am I realizing the best that is in me or the worst? My will to keep on striving is being broken. I doubt the worth of my action. When I see him so unhappy I say to myself: 'Have you the right?' and I find no answer to satisfy me. I can only argue and argue until my brain aches. How can I bear hardship for a cause in which my faith is wavering? That is why I come to you."

ROYLSTON. (*in a troubled voice*) "I cannot tell you how deeply grieved I am to have been even the indirect means of causing you pain."

MRS. FRAZER. (*excitedly*) "I have the right to come to you, haven't I? Mentally I am your creation. That you had no knowledge of my existence when you wrote does not lessen your responsibility in my eyes. I demand that you restore my peace of mind by justifying me to myself."

ROYLSTON. (*deeply moved*) "What I have written cannot apply to every case." (*with conviction*) "But it is my sincerest belief that you have found yourself, that as things stand between you, it would be folly for you to go back to your husband; that out of your present distress will spring a higher satisfaction than you have ever before known or believed possible. Therefore I urge you not to give up the battle, for in the end you will achieve a victory well worth the winning."

MRS. FRAZER. (*extending both her hands to him - gratefully*) "You have given me new hope, new strength."

ROYLSTON. (*taking her hands and looking into her eyes*) "Promise me you will call on me whenever you need help in the future."

MRS. FRAZER. (*withdrawing her hands - simply*) "I promise to do so."

ROYLSTON. (*smiling*) "You must now, you know. You have charged me with the responsibility. You must let me pay off my debt."

MRS. FRAZER. (*forcing a smile*) "Whenever my supply of will-power runs low I'll come a-borrowing, never fear."

ROYLSTON. "By the way, I meant to ask you if your mother and brother know anything of all this?"

MRS. FRAZER. "No. My mother is in Switzerland. Her health is so feeble I have not dared to tell her about it; and I know she would never learn of it through Mr. Frazer. My brother is the manager of a railroad in Brazil and very seldom returns to this county or writes to me. So, of course, he knows nothing."

ROYLSTON. "But your husband's family?"

MRS. FRAZER. "I believe he has told them something about my being in California for my health."

ROYLSTON. "You have that in your favor. Family inter- ference always complicates matters. As for the position I prom- ised you, I will see what I can do when I go to the city in the morning. I have many influential friends and I have no doubt a real opportunity will be found for you someplace. In the meantime I have lots of work which should be typewritten and if you care to - "

MRS. FRAZER. "Oh, how good of you! Your encourage- ment has made me feel so hopeful, so full of energy, I am ready for anything. A new life of wonderful possibilities seems open- ing up before me."

ROYLSTON. "It will be full of obstacles, too."

MRS. FRAZER. (*spiritedly*) "The harder the better. With your help I know I shall overcome them."

ROYLSTON. "You are overrating me. Take warning!"

MRS. FRAZER. (*picking up her hat from the sofa*) "And now I had better be going back to my little hall room."

ROYLSTON. (*looking at his watch - then turning to her with a quizzical smile*) "Yes, but how?"

MRS. FRAZER. "What do you mean?"

ROYLSTON. "I mean the little hall-room will have to remain

empty tonight. You have missed the last train."

MRS. FRAZER. (*apparently greatly astonished*) "Surely you don't mean it? And I never looked at the timetable! Why didn't you warn me?"

ROYLSTON. "I had no idea what time it was."

MRS. FRAZER. "How stupid of me! That comes of living in the city where you can always get the Subway or something. I must get back some way."

ROYLSTON. "It's impossible, I'm afraid."

MRS. FRAZER. "Then what can I do?"

ROYLSTON. "You must stay here."

MRS. FRAZER. "Here - in this house?"

ROYLSTON. "There is no alternative unless you wish to pass the night in the fields."

MRS. FRAZER. "There must be a hotel."

ROYLSTON. "There is only a roadhouse, a place of very questionable character, frequented by joy-riders and their - companions. You could not go there; and I know of no other place. You see, there are nothing but summer residences around here and I am hardly acquainted with any of the neighbors." (*gravely*) "Think of the time of night, and the rain, of the conclusions which would be drawn. You are beautiful and people have evil minds. Don't you see the impossibility?"

MRS. FRAZER. "Yes - but, oh - how can I stay here? What will your wife think?"

ROYLSTON. "She will not think. She will never know."

MRS. FRAZER. "I - I don't understand."

ROYLSTON. "She is not here. Except for the servants I am all alone."

MRS. FRAZER. (*genuinely alarmed*) "Then I must go, even if I do have to spend the night in the fields."

ROYLSTON. "Listen; there is rather a strange coincidence, or shall I say fatality in all this. My wife went with the children to see the fairy play in New York, and contrary to her usual custom - she doesn't care for motoring - she went down in the machine. Otherwise I could have had the chauffeur drive you home; but they won't return before tomorrow afternoon at the earliest."

MRS. FRAZER. (*frightened*) "This is terrible. How can I - " (*hurries to the window and looks out*) "It's pouring."

ROYLSTON. "Fatality."

MRS. FRAZER. (*imploringly*) "Please, please suggest something! You know I can't stay." (*She looks at him pleadingly - her lips tremble.*)

ROYLSTON. "Why not?" (*slowly*) "Don't you believe you would be as safe here in my house as in your dingy hall bedroom?"

MRS. FRAZER. (*looking at him searchingly*) "Yes - I know I would be - but - "

ROYLSTON. (*impatiently*) "But you are afraid of appearances, of what people might think if they knew. You never learned that fear from me. Is not the knowledge of your own innocence enough to raise you above such considerations? Or are you afraid I may be a Don Juan in disguise?"

MRS. FRAZER. "No, I am not afraid of you."

ROYLSTON. "And even if you fear appearances? Who is to know?"

MRS. FRAZER. (*wavering*) "You forget your servant."

ROYLSTON. "He has been with me for years, was with my father before me, all his life has been in our service. I flatter myself he's a model of discretion."

MRS. FRAZER. "But what will he think of me?" (*seeing Roylston's scornful smile*) "But it doesn't matter. I will stay."

ROYLSTON. "Bravo! It would be foolish and cowardly of you to get soaked with the rain and be insulted, and perhaps worse, in the railroad station for the sake of a worn-out code of ethics."

MRS. FRAZER. (*smiling feebly*) "Your wife might not think the ethics worn out."

ROYLSTON. (*carelessly*) "Oh, my wife; she would not think anything. If it would ease your conscience, I will tell her the whole thing. I'm sure she'd forget all about it ten minutes later" (*contemptuously*) "when the butcher came for his order."

MRS. FRAZER. (*impulsively*) "You do not love your wife, do you?" (*as Roylston looks at her in astonishment, she grows confused*) "What an impertinent question! Forgive me!"

ROYLSTON. (*lightly*) "So impertinent I never dare ask it of myself. I have always rejected the temptation to analyze my home relations. They are pleasant enough and that is all I care to know."

MRS. FRAZER. (*with a sad smile*) "If I had looked at it that way - "

ROYLSTON. "The family relationship was the most important thing in the world for you at that time. With me it is purely secondary. My work comes first. As long as my home life gives free scope for my creative faculty I will demand nothing further of it. Life is too meager, too stingy with its favors, for us to ask for perfection. So I accept my domestic bliss at its surface value and save my analytical eye for the creations of my brain."

(*smiling*) "I see you are vainly trying to stifle a yawn, and I know you must be terribly tired and sleepy. Won't you let me direct you to your room?" (*He goes to the door on left.*)

MRS. FRAZER. (*forgetting her hat which she leaves lying on the sofa, smilingly walks over to him*) "I am dismissed, then?"

ROYLSTON. "Far from it. I merely wish to save you the embarrassment of falling asleep in the chair." (*pointing*) "You see the light at the top of the stairway? Well, turn to your left when you reach the top and boldly enter the first room on your left. You will find everything there you need, I imagine. It is the official number one guest chamber."

MRS. FRAZER. "I suppose you won't retire for hours yet?"

ROYLSTON. "I have some work to finish up."

MRS. FRAZER. (*catching herself in the act of yawning - with a laugh*) "I can't deny I'm sleepy - for the first time in months." (*giving him her hand*) "If you only knew how grateful I am! How can I ever thank you?"

ROYLSTON. (*with sudden passion*) "By looking at me like that. How beautiful you are!"

MRS. FRAZER. (*withdrawing her hand - a note of warning in her voice*) "Remember the Princess in the fairy tales who was as good as - "

ROYLSTON. "She was beautiful. I understand. Pardon me. Good - but emancipated."

MRS. FRAZER. (*smiling*) "Free to be good." (*She turns to go out the door.*)

ROYLSTON. "Good night." (*goes toward the table.*)

MRS. FRAZER. (*turns to him suddenly, a look of resolution on her face*) "I must explain one thing before I go, before I accept your hospitality. I have told you a lie; (*Roylston looks at her in surprise*) "I never met you at the studio ball. I was there but I did not meet you. I knew I had missed the last train. That is the reason I came so late. I wanted to miss it. And I knew there was no hotel for I made inquiries at the station. But I had no idea your wife would be away."

ROYLSTON. (*staring at her in amazement*) "But why, why?"

MRS. FRAZER. "I wanted to put you to the test, to see if you would help me and let me stay. I wanted to get a glimpse of your home life, to see if you were a real man with the courage of your convictions or just a theorist." (*hesitatingly*) "You see in my agony of doubt it seemed necessary for me to get back of dry words to a flesh and blood reality." (*with a faint smile*) "It all appears such a wild idea now; and the test turned out to be a test of myself after all, didn't it?"

ROYLSTON. (*not able to recover from his astonishment*) "You tell me this - now - that you purposely missed the last train?"

MRS. FRAZER. (*flushing*) "I am ashamed to say that is the exact truth." (*avoiding his ardent gaze*) "I wish there to be no deception on my part after all your kindness to me."

ROYLSTON. (*intensely*) "Do you realize how beautiful you are? Are you not afraid to make such a confession to me - of the conclusions I might be vain enough to draw from it?" (*He moves a step toward her.*)

MRS. FRAZER. (*looking straight into his eyes*) "No - because I know now you *are* a real man."

ROYLSTON. (*moving still nearer to her*) "Take care! The real men are usually the greatest sinners."

MRS. FRAZER. "But they protect the helpless." (*with a smile*) "So you see how safe I am. Good night." (*She goes out.*)

ROYLSTON. (*going to the door*) "Good night" (*He watches her ascend the stairway*) "Good night." (*He comes back and sits down at the table again; starts to look over his manuscript, glances upward in the direction of her room, throws his manuscript down with an exclamation of disgust, goes to the door on the left again and looks up at the top of the stairway, finally comes back to the table again and stands beside it for a moment, frowning thoughtfully and evidently weighing something in his mind.*) "Damnation!" (*He takes his hat and light overcoat from the chair, puts them on, grabs his cane and hurries out through the door at the back as*

THE CURTAIN FALLS

"SERVITUDE" - ACT II

ACT II. The same - about nine o'clock the following morning.

SCENE. *The same. It is about nine o'clock on the following morning. Bright sunlight streams in through the two open windows. Benton is arranging the papers and books on the table. Having finished he turns and is going out the door in the rear when he catches sight of Mrs. Frazer's hat which is lying on the sofa. He gives a low whistle of amazement. A shadow falls across the sunlight at one of the windows and a moment later Weson, the gardener, puts his head into the room and peers around near-sightedly. He is an old withered man with a drooping gray mustache stained yellow by tobacco juice.*

BENTON. "Good morning, Weson."

WESON. "Oh, it's you, is it?"

BENTON. "Who did you think it was?"

WESON. "I thought maybe Mr. Roylston -"

BENTON. "He isn't up yet. Want to see him about anything?"

WESON. "Nothin' special. When I first come out this mornin' I seen a feller hangin' round the house s'picious like. Soon s'he seen me he turned round and walked off s'fast s'he could go. 'D'you think this is a park?' I shouts after him, but he didn't pay no attention. Thinks I: I better tell Mr. Roylston about you. With all them burglaries happenin' nearabouts you can't be too careful."

BENTON. "Hm - you're right about that." (*With an involuntary glance at the hat*) "Mr. Roylston ought to be more careful."

WESON. "Oughter hire a watchman, s'what I say." (*In a whining voice*) "T'ain't safe for me sleepin' all alone in that house at the end of the drive. S'me they'd tackle first. I was readin' in the papers t'other day where robbers tortured an old gardener same s'me to make him tell them how to git into the house; burned his bare feet with a red-hot poker!" (*With rising inflection*) "Ain't that turrible?"

BENTON. "Oh, I guess you're safe enough." (*Meaningly*) "It isn't burglars his nibs ought to be frightened of."

WESON. (*Eagerly, scenting a scandal*) "What's he been up to now?"

BENTON. (*Picks up Mrs. Frazer's hat*) "Cast your eye on this."

WESON. "Wait till I git my specs." (*Reaches into his pocket and pulls out a pair of steel-rimmed spectacles*) "I can't see nothin' without 'em no more." (*Puts them on and looks at the hat, - in disappointed tones*) "What's that? One of the Missus' hats?"

BENTON. "Guess again. She don't wear cheap truck like that." (*Throws hat contemptuously on sofa.*)

WESON. "You don't mean -?" (*With an explosive chuckle*) "If he don't beat the devil! An' the Missus in Noo York! Makes hay while the sun shines, don't he? Don't the Missus never guess nothin'?"

BENTON. (*Scornfully*) "She doesn't know enough; besides usually he chucks 'em before the thing gets serious. He likes to have them crazy about him but when they get too mushy - he doesn't like complications - they interfere with his work, he says; and then when they call up I have to say he's too busy to be disturbed."

WESON. (*Admiringly*) "Foxy, ain't he?"

BENTON. "I don't know what's wrong with him this time. I don't blame him, though; she's a beauty. But he ought to be more careful. Once caught, twice shy, they say; and he was caught once, good and proper." (*With a short laugh*) "It'll do the Missus good to get a dose of her own medicine. It broke the old man's heart when the young fellow married her, and -" (*Stopping abruptly as he sees how avidly Weson is drinking his words in*) "A fine man to work for, the old gentleman; not that I'm complaining of the son at all."

WESON. "What was you sayin' about the marriage?"

BENTON. "Nothing that an old scandalmonger like you ought to hear. There's lots of things I could tell if I had a mind to; but I'll keep my mouth shut. It's the best policy, Weson, especially when you're around. You better get out of here. I think I hear someone coming down the stairs." (*Weson hurriedly withdraws. Benton goes to the table and pretends to be arranging the things on it. Mrs. Frazer appears in the doorway on the left. She stops uncertainly when she sees Benton.*)

BENTON. (*Affably*) "Good morning, ma'am."

MRS. FRAZER. (*Embarrassed*) "Good morning. I believe I left my hat in here."

BENTON. "Yes, ma'am. Here it is." (*He picks her hat from the sofa.*)

MRS. FRAZER. (*Walking over and taking it from him*) "Thank you." (*She goes to the window and stands drinking in the beauty of the Spring morning*)

BENTON. (*With an admiring glance at her figure framed in the sunlight*) "Beautiful morning, ma'am."

MRS. FRAZER. "Yes, isn't it? And what a lovely garden."

BENTON. "Yes, ma'am, very fine. It has the gardener busy all the time keeping it in shape."

MRS. FRAZER. "No doubt; they require a great deal of care. Has Mr. Roylston come down yet?"

BENTON. "Lord no, ma'am; won't be down for an hour

yet, I should say. He's not what you'd call an early bird; stays up so late nights he couldn't be." (*Insinuatingly*) "But he's been so queer and - hm - different from what he usually does, he might do anything this morning."

MRS. FRAZER. (*Crushing him with a look of icy hauteur*) "What do you mean?"

BENTON. (*Confused, fumbling with the books on the table*) "Nothing at all, ma'am, only -"

MRS. FRAZER. (*Her curiosity getting the better of her - more kindly*) "Only what?"

BENTON. (*Accepting her change of manner as a confession which equalizes their position*) "Only, begging your pardon, he doesn't usually - he isn't in the habit of - he usually thinks that sort of thing too dangerous. Now, when the others -"

· MRS. FRAZER. (*Horrified*) "Others?"

BENTON. (*Grinning*) "Loads of 'em. They're all crazy about him. He likes it, too - phone calls and letters and flowers and all such stuff. He pretends not to care, but it tickles him just the same to have them adoring him, asking for his advice -"

MRS. FRAZER. "Stop! Is this the way you slander the man who trusts you?"

BENTON. (*Offended*) "It's no secret. He laughs and talks about it himself. I've heard him read parts of the letters to the Missus, Mrs. Roylston. I was only saying it to you because it's never - he's never taken any chances for the others. I thought you'd like to know you were the only one -"

MRS. FRAZER. (*Her face crimson*) "How dare you!"

BENTON. (*Quickly*) "Beg your pardon, ma'am, no offence intended." (*Slyly*) "Of course I don't mean anything wrong." (*The sound of a door closing is heard from the hallway on the left, then children's voices. Benton turns excitedly to Mrs. Frazer)* "Good Gawd, it must be Mrs. Roylston and the kids. Go in there where she won't see you." *(Mrs. Frazer, too overcome with fear and shame to stop and think, hurries through the door at the rear. Benton closes it after her and is busy with the papers on the table when Mrs. Roylston enters with the children who are talking and laughing together.)*

Mrs. Roylston is a pretty woman of thirty or so, with a mass of light curly brown hair, big thoughtful eyes, rosy complexion, tiny hands and feet, and a slight girlish figure. She is dressed stylishly but without ostentation.

Davie and Ruth, aged nine and seven respectively, are healthy, noisy, delightful children. Their clothes are simple but of expensive material.)

MRS. ROYLSTON. "Good morning, Benton. Mr. Roylston's not up yet of course?"

BENTON. "No. ma'am."

MRS. ROYLSTON. "Telephone for Dr. Morse at once, will you, Benton? Tell him to come up at once."

BENTON. "Yes, ma'am. Nothing serious, I hope ma'am."

MRS. ROYLSTON. "Oh no. Ruth was ill last night when we returned from the theatre. Mrs. Dexter sent for her doctor. He said it was nothing but -" *(Smiling and shaking an accusing finger at Ruth)* "too much candy. However, I wanted to make sure. I have no confidence in strange doctors. So I took the first train out this morning and didn't wait for the machine."

RUTH. "I did'n eat much, Mother."

DAVIE. "I ate more'n she did, and I was'n sick."

MRS. ROYLSTON. "But you're a man, dear."

RUTH. "I feel puffictly well this morning, Mother."

MRS. ROYLSTON. (*Kissing her*) "Of course you do, dear. Mother wishes to make sure, that's all. So telephone right away, please, Benton."

BENTON. "Yes, ma'am." (*With an apprehensive glance at the door in back he hurries out to the left.*)

DAVIE. "Mother, can we go out and play in the sand-pile?"

RUTH. "I'm goin' to play I'm the Princess in the play last night."

MRS. ROYLSTON. "And are you going to be the Prince, Davie?"

DAVIE. "Nope; I'm goin' to be the dragon."

MRS. ROYLSTON. "But the dragon was very, very wicked."

DAVIE. "Tha's why I wanta be him."

MRS. ROYLSTON. (*Laughing and kissing both of them*) "Run along then, and be sure and stay in the sun; and come in when you see Dr. Morse drive up. Try and be as quiet as you can. You know your father isn't up yet." (*The children answer: "Yes, Mother" and skip out through the door on the left.*)

BENTON. (*Appears in the doorway on the left*) "Dr. Morse will be right up, ma'am."

MRS. ROYLSTON. "Very well. Thank you, Benton." (*Benton, unwilling to leave the room, and not knowing any excuse for remaining, stands fidgetting nervously in the doorway.*) "Anything you wish to see me about, Benton?"

BENTON. "No, ma'am, nothing at all. So glad to hear it's not serious - Miss Ruth, I mean."

MRS. ROYLSTON. (*Smiling at him kindly*) "Thank you, Benton" (*She sits down and picking up the manuscript from the table, starts to read. Benton turns reluctantly and leaves. Mrs. Roylston glances over the pages of the manuscript inter-*

estedly. The door in the rear is slowly opened and Mrs. Frazer comes into the room. Her face wears an expression of defiant shame. She coughs to attract Mrs. Roylston's attention. Startled by the sound, Mrs. Roylston turns around and sees her. The two women stare at each other in silence for a moment. Mrs. Roylston grows very pale. Her lips tremble and it seems as if she were shrinking up in her chair, becoming small and pitiful. A flush slowly spreads over Mrs. Frazer's face. She drops her eyes.)

MRS. FRAZER. "I beg your pardon."

MRS. ROYLSTON. "How did - Who is it you wish to see?"

MRS. FRAZER. "I am waiting to speak to Mr. Roylston."

MRS. ROYLSTON. "How did you get in that room?"

MRS. FRAZER. (*Defiantly*) "I hid there when I heard you coming."

MRS. ROYLSTON. (*With a sigh that is like a moan*) "I knew it! I knew it!"

MRS. FRAZER. (*Embarrassed*) "I lost my head completely for a moment, and I ran away. I was so afraid of what you might think. In there I regained my senses. I had done no wrong. Why should I be afraid of you? So I came back."

MRS. ROYLSTON. (*Slowly*) "I am the one who should be afraid."

MRS. FRAZER. "I was sure you would misunderstand my presence here."

MRS. ROYLSTON. (*Coldly*) "I'm afraid I understand it only too well."

MRS. FRAZER. "Mr. Roylston was so positive you would ignore appearances. I knew better. I am a woman. I should never have allowed myself to be persuaded into remaining here against my better judgement."

MRS. ROYLSTON. (*Trying not to understand*) "Mr. Roylston? You have seen him? Is he up already?"

MRS. FRAZER. (*Unflinchingly*) "No; I saw him last night."

MRS. ROYLSTON. "Last night? Then you - When did you come here-"

MRS. FRAZER. "Last night about ten o'clock."

MRS. ROYLSTON. (*Her worst fears realized*) "Last night? Ten o'clock? Then you were here in this house - you and he - alone?"

MRS. FRAZER. "Yes; but you must not draw any conclusions from that until I -"

MRS. ROYLSTON. (*Jumping to her feet, her eyes flashing*) "Oh!"

MRS. FRAZER. "You will be sorry if you form a hasty judgement."

MRS. ROYLSTON. "Hasty? As if I had not always a picture of this before my mind! I have known it was coming, dreaded it, for years. Hasty? Oh no! I have prayed this would never happen, but I have seen it drawing nearer every day in spite of my prayers; and I am prepared for it."

MRS. FRAZER. "If you will permit me to explain -"

MRS. ROYLSTON. (*With a mocking laugh*) "Explain!"

MRS. FRAZER. (*Firmly*) "I came here to ask your husband's advice."

MRS. ROYLSTON. "They all want advice - so they say."

MRS. FRAZER. (*Flushing angrily but controlling herself*) "I was in such desperate straits that only he could help me. I was wild with despair. I formed the mad idea of coming here. I never thought of your being away. And I missed the last train." (*She realizes how improbable this explanation must seem to Mrs.*

Roylston and continues uncertainly) "There was no hotel to go to; so your husband kindly -"

MRS. ROYLSTON. (*Her laughter breaking hysterically*) "And you expect me to believe this! Do you think I have no intelligence at all?" (*Furiously*) "Lies! Lies! All lies! (*Throwing herself in the chair by the table she sobs convulsively, her face hidden in her hands.*)

MRS. FRAZER. (*Calmly*) "I will excuse your insults because I know how you must feel." (*Earnestly*) "You will regret this when the truth comes out, when you know you have been insulting an innocent woman. You are judging by appearances and letting them deceive you."

MRS. ROYLSTON. "Lies, lies! Haven't I read your letters to him?"

MRS. FRAZER. (*Astonished*) "I never wrote to your husband in my life."

MRS. ROYLSTON. (*As if she hadn't heard*) " 'Will you give me permission to come out and see you sometime?' I suppose you never wrote that? Oh, how well I remember them - those letters!"

MRS. FRAZER. "Mrs. Roylston, you are mistaken. I never -"

MRS. ROYLSTON. "To take advantage of my being away with the children; oh, how could he!"

MRS. FRAZER. "Mrs. Roylston, you must listen to me."

MRS. ROYLSTON. "I won't listen to you. What is there to say - now? You love him. I don't blame you for that; but what will become of me? (*She breaks down and sobs unrestrainedly.*)

MRS. FRAZER. (*Waiting until Mrs. R. has regained control of herself*) "Listen to me, Mrs. Roylston! I do not love your husband."

MRS. ROYLSTON. "The more shame, then; for he must love you."

MRS. FRAZER. "He never saw me before last night."

MRS. ROYLSTON. (*Coldly*) "I don't believe you."

MRS. FRAZER. (*Angrily*) "Ah, there is a limit to everything. Since you persist in insulting me, since you refuse to listen to anything, you may continue to believe whatever you please. I will leave Mr. Roylston to do the explaining." (*She hurries toward the door on the left but Mrs. R. jumps up and reaches it before her, blocking her passage.*)

MRS. ROYLSTON. (*Fiercely*) "You cannot go now."

MRS. FRAZER. "Cannot?"

MRS. ROYLSTON. "I don't mean that. Please don't go yet, before he comes. There is so much which must be cleared up. I didn't mean to hurt you. If you knew how I am suffering you wouldn't blame me. Please sit down, won't you, until he comes?"

MRS. FRAZER. (*On the verge of tears herself*) "After the things you have said to me? No, I will not remain in this house a minute longer. Please let me pass."

MRS. ROYLSTON. "I am sorry. You are not to blame. No one is to blame. I implore you to stay until he comes. He ought to be down in a few minutes. It won't be long."

MRS. FRAZER. (*After a moment's indecision*) "Very well, I will stay; not because you ask me to but because I wish to hear my own justification." (*She sits down in one of the armchairs near the sofa.*)

MRS. ROYLSTON. "Thank you. It will help to clear up matters between the three of us once and for all." (*She chokes back a sob and sits down in the chair by the table.*)

MRS. FRAZER. "In the meantime, if you please, let us not talk about it. It will only make matters worse - if that were possible."

MRS. ROYLSTON. (*Strangely*) "How you said that! As if you were giving an order. And why shouldn't you? You have more right in this house than I have." (*She sobs.*)

MRS. FRAZER. (*Moved in spite of herself - with great kindness*) "Please, Mrs. Roylston, don't make yourself unhappy in this way. If you only knew how wrong you are."

MRS. ROYLSTON. (*More calmly*) "I won't break down again. What must be, must be I suppose. I have known this was coming for a long time. The day I was married I could foresee it. I should have had the courage to refuse then; but I didn't. It all seemed such a wonderful dream come true, I just couldn't refuse even when I knew I was wronging him. I was a coward then and I still am, I guess. Eleven years of happiness and now I have to pay and - I am afraid." (*A pause during which Mrs. F. looks at her pityingly*) "I've pretended not to see a lot of things in those years. I wanted him to be happy, and I knew he wouldn't be if he thought he had a jealous wife prying into his affairs. All the women who sent him flowers and wrote to him and called him up on the phone - I knew they loved him, and I hated them for it; but I never let him think I suspected anything. Until lately I never thought he considered them seriously."

MRS. FRAZER. (*Interrupting her indignantly*) "And you think I was one of those fools!"

MRS. ROYLSTON. "He used to read parts of their letters to me. He never guessed how it hurt. For I could see in spite of the way he joked they pleased him just the same. Then all at once he stopped showing them to me - and they kept coming, all in the same handwriting. I had never read a letter of his before but I brooded until I couldn't resist the temptation any longer. Two of them were lying open on this table one day and I read them. Then I could see the end coming. He had been writing to her, meeting her in New York, and I knew from her letters it was only a question of time."

MRS. FRAZER. "And those are the letters you think I wrote?"

MRS. ROYLSTON. (*Dully*) "Yes."

MRS. FRAZER. "But when I swear to you I never wrote a line to your husband in my life, never spoke a word to him before last night!"

MRS. ROYLSTON. "I'd like to believe you." (*Intensely*) "Oh, I wish I could believe you! But how can I?"

MRS. FRAZER. (*Desperately*) "You will have to. He will tell you the same thing."

MRS. ROYLSTON. (*Her voice low and shaken with pain*) "What does it matter? You or someone else. She said she had left her home to work out her own salvation; and I thought you looked that way. I thought she would be younger. Her letters sounded girlish. What does it matter? *You* were here - last night."

MRS. FRAZER. (*Quietly*) "Mrs. Roylston, I really cannot stay and listen to such implications."

MRS. ROYLSTON. "I don't blame you or anyone. It's my own sin coming back on me. Marriages like mine are cursed."

MRS. FRAZER. "Cursed? It seems to me yours has been a very fortunate one."

MRS. ROYLSTON. "Yes, cursed. Sooner or later the curse falls. Retribution finds you out in the end. Forbidden love - you'll find out the curse of it like I have, when you least expect it, when you think you're happy and the future is all smiling."

MRS. FRAZER. (*Interested*) "I fail to see how all this can apply to your case."

MRS. ROYLSTON. (*Continues in a lifeless, monotonous voice as if all the spirit in her had been crushed and broken. Her face wears an expression of dazed, almost stupid, resignation*) "Give him up before it's too late, for your own sake. You'll have to pay. I'll be frank with you. You can't throw any stone. He married me because he had to, or thought he had to. I was his father's stenographer, we loved each other - too well. His father found out and discharged me. Then David asked me to marry him and I couldn't refuse. I loved him so."

MRS. FRAZER. (*Bewildered*) "Please, Mrs. Roylston, don't -"

MRS. ROYLSTON. "I want you to understand - whatever happens to me afterwards - it isn't his fault."

MRS. FRAZER. "Do you know what you are telling me?"

MRS. ROYLSTON. (*Hotly*) "I wouldn't be ashamed to tell it to the whole world. It shows how good he is. If he no longer loves me it's because I allowed him to make too great a sacrifice. His father cut him off and never spoke to him again. The old gentleman was kind enough generally but he had great plans for his only son, David, and I spoilt them all. He died soon afterward, - of grief over our marriage, they say. I've always thought that perhaps in his heart David has never forgiven me for - killing his father."

MRS. FRAZER. "How can you imagine such a thing?"

MRS. ROYLSTON. "When I married him I resolved that as soon as he was able to take care of himself -"

MRS. FRAZER. (*Astonished*) "Take care of himself?"

MRS. ROYLSTON. "He wasn't famous in those days. He hadn't even had a book published yet. He used to take positions in offices but he never held them long and I could see how he hated them. He wanted to write, write, write all the time. Every once in a while he sold an article, but not often enough to keep him alive. It must have been terribly hard for him - worrying and fretting how to make two ends meet. He had been accustomed to everything he wanted - and I had dragged him down. He wouldn't have been human if he hadn't had a sort of grudge against me for it."

MRS. FRAZER. "He is hardly as mean as that."

MRS. ROYLSTON. "I had to stay with him until he got on his feet. I was considered a fine stenographer in those days and my salary was enough to keep us going. Then, too, he had to have someone to typewrite his manuscripts for him."

MRS. FRAZER. (*With wondering admiration*) "And you did all that?"

MRS. ROYLSTON. "I had plenty of time at night to typewrite what he had written during the day. Those were the happiest days of my life. How often since then I've wished that he had never been successful, that we could have gone on like that always. It was selfish of me to feel that way but I couldn't help it sometimes." (*Musingly*) "We had a small flat all to ourselves."

MRS. FRAZER. "And you did all the housekeeping, too?"

MRS. ROYLSTON. (*Simply*) "Of course. I had made a resolve to leave him and let him get a divorce as soon as he was successful and could get along without me. I saw clearly at that time, before the children came, what I see now - that he was never meant for me. I knew he would come to regret his sacrifice and I would become a dead weight holding him back. I knew nothing of what he knew. Whatever I have learned since, he has taught me. We had been married a little over a year when his first play was produced and made a sensation, - and then -"

MRS. FRAZER. (*Eagerly*) "Yes?"

MRS. ROYLSTON. (*Softly*) "Little Davie came. I couldn't think of going away then. It would have killed me. I wasn't strong enough or brave enough for that. I hoped he would love me more for Davie's sake, and he did for a time. He was so kind to me; and when our little girl was born he was so proud. As he became famous he had less and less time to spend at home, and he hated to be disturbed when he was writing. He met so many people, women, of his own kind outside, who could talk about the things he was interested in, that I guess he commenced to despise me a little because I was so stupid."

MRS. FRAZER. (*With a strange smile, half to herself*) "No, no, he has never analyzed his home relations."

MRS. ROYLSTON. (*As if she had not heard*) "Lately he has grown more and more indifferent to me and to the children; so that now I'm afraid he only looks on me as a sort of house-keeper." (*With a pitiful attempt at a smile*) "He'll have to acknowledge I'm a good one. I've protected him from all the small worries he detests so much. I don't believe he realizes; he thinks things just run along by themselves."

MRS. FRAZER. (*Eagerly*) "Why have you never asserted your-self, claimed your right as an individual? Why have you never spoken to him, told him how you felt? You have seen him slipping away and made no attempt to hold him."

MRS. ROYLSTON. (*Fiercely*) "I have loved him, loved him, loved him with all my heart and soul; loved him more than you or any other woman will ever love him. If that has no power to hold him, - then I have lost him."

MRS. FRAZER. (*After a pause*) "How unhappy you must have been!"

MRS. ROYLSTON. (*Scornfully*) "Unhappy? So that's what

you think! How little you know! I have been happy in serving him, happy in the knowledge that I have had my little part in helping him to success, happy to be able to shield and protect him. In spite of all you other women with your letters and flowers, I have been happy." (*With a sad smile*) "However, it's all ended now. As long as I could pretend I didn't know about you others, as long as I was sure he didn't suspect I knew about you, I could remain and love him and still preserve my self-respect. It's different now. I can't pretend to be blind any longer. I know, and you know I know, and he knows I know. Besides I see that his future happiness does not depend on me and" (*Intensely*) "above all else in the world I want him to be happy."

MRS. FRAZER. "But he *is* happy - now - with you!"

MRS. ROYLSTON. (*Shaking her head sadly*) "My usefullness is past. I can only thank God for granting the beauty and joy of the past eleven years to a woman who sinned and was too cowardly to pay. The payment was never cancelled, only post-poned, I see that now - postponed until I had the courage to pay. I have that courage now. I will pay. I will leave him to his happiness." (*Her voice thrilling with pride*) "How many of you others love him as much as that? Not many, or one, I think. How many of you would make the sacrifice I will make? How many of you would be willing to give him up to another woman because your love was so great? Not one of you!" (*Bitterly*) "You the least of all - for him or anyone else! I can see it in your face."

MRS. FRAZER. (*Slowly*) "It is true. Compared to you I am a weakling."

MRS. ROYLSTON. "I do not boast of my strength, only of the strength of my love. I thank you just the same. You are the only person who has ever given me credit for being what I must be. Not even he ever saw it in all these eleven years."

MRS. FRAZER. "But did you ever lay bare your soul to anyone, even to him, as you have to me?"

MRS. ROYLSTON. "Yes, to him, every day, every hour; but he never saw it."

MRS. FRAZER. (*After a pause - thoughtfully*) "How much you have taught me! Happiness, then, means servitude?"

MRS. ROYLSTON. "Love means servitude; and *my* love is *my* happiness."

MRS. FRAZER. "I should have come to you for advice, not to him."

MRS. ROYLSTON. (*With a scornful smile*) "Advice? That word has been my torturer. You women of the flowers and letters have stolen him from me in the name of advice."

MRS. FRAZER. (*Hurt*) "Even now you have no faith in me."

MRS. ROYLSTON. "It isn't possible. How can I? How can I?"

MRS. FRAZER. "I can't blame you; things are so mixed. It must appear incredible. But can't you see that I, too, have suffered? Even if what you think were true could you not pity me?"

MRS. ROYLSTON. (*Excitedly*) "No, no, no, I can only hate you. How can the vanquished pity the victor? You ask too much."

MRS. FRAZER. (*Rising from her chair*) "I cannot wait any longer. I must go out into the fresh air and be alone for a while - to think."

MRS. ROYLSTON. "You are afraid to wait until he comes."

MRS. FRAZER. "I will wait outside. In this room the weight of your suspicion is crushing me. I begin to feel guilty."

MRS. ROYLSTON. (*Savagely*) "Ah!"

MRS. FRAZER. (*Weakly*) "I will wait outside in the garden if I may." (*She starts to go. The sound of a door slamming is heard. Mrs. Roylston goes to the door on the left and looks out. She gives an exclamation of surprise.*)

MRS. ROYLSTON. (*Slowly*) "He has just come in. He must have been out for his morning walk. What could have got him up so early?" (*Turns impetuously to Mrs. Frazer*) "You must have known of this; and you wanted to sneak away before he came. Lies! Lies! Lies everywhere!"

MRS. FRAZER. (*Distractedly*) "No, no, I swear to you -"

MRS. ROYLSTON. "Ssshh! Here he comes." (*Roylston enters from the door on the left. He is dressed exactly the same as the night before.*)

ROYLSTON. (*Concealing his annoyance*) "Hello, Alice, what brings you back at this unearthly hour? Good morning, Mrs. Frazer."

MRS. ROYLSTON. (*Falteringly*) "Ruth was sick last night and I didn't wait for the machine this morning but hurried out on the first train. She seems to be all right this morning but I've sent for Dr. Morse to make sure."

ROYLSTON. (*Indifferently, shrugging his shoulders*) "Stuffed full of candy, probably. I see you and Mrs. Frazer have already made each other's acquaintance."

MRS. ROYLSTON. (*With a short laugh at what she thinks is his attempt to deceive her in the name*) "Oh, yes." (*Mrs. Frazer does not reply but stares at him as if she were seeing him for the first time.*)

ROYLSTON. (*Searching through the things on the table*) "God be thanked I haven't a jealous wife; for I must acknowledge that even to the most unprejudiced observer the events of last night would appear dubious." (*Irritably*) "Where did Benton put - ? Oh, here it is." (*Finds the fountain pen he has been looking for and puts it in his pocket*) "You see Mrs. Frazer missed the last train and when I explained that you were away it was all I could do to persuade her to occupy Guest Chamber No. 1 instead of melting to death in the rain. Nice situation, wasn't it? Nothing if not compromising. Married man, married lady - not to each other - lonely country house - stormy night - wife returns home unexpectedly the next morning and - does not believe the worst." (*With a laugh which has a trace of mockery in it*) "My dear Alice, you are really the perfect wife." (*Goes over to her and puts his arm around her carelessly and continues in the same bantering tone*) "I told you, Mrs. Frazer, that Caesar's wife was above harboring suspicion. I welcome you to the model household, where truth reigns, where conventions are as naught, where we believe in each other implicitly because we have found each other so worthy of belief. And I salute you, My Angel of Trustfulness." (*He bends to kiss his wife. She gently pushes him away.*)

MRS. ROYLSTON. "Don't, David, please!"

ROYLSTON. (*Glancing from one to the other. Mrs. Frazer is looking at him with frank disgust*) "Hm - I was too hasty in my reliance on mutual confidence it seems. You two have had a run-in already, I see." (*To his wife, impatiently*) "I am sorry you should have jumped at conclusions before you heard my explanation. Mrs. Frazer is going to do some work for me and -"

MRS. ROYLSTON. (*Her eyes filling*) "Ah."

ROYLSTON. "Which will necessitate her being here for some time, and we must clear away all unpleasantness -"

MRS. FRAZER. (*Interrupting him coldly*) "You are mistaken.

I have decided I cannot accept the work you offer me.''

ROYLSTON. (*Perplexed*) "Hm, - it's as bad as that, eh?''

MRS. ROYLSTON. (*Turning to Mrs. Frazer*) "But you must!''

MRS. FRAZER. (*Indignantly*) "Must?''

MRS. ROYLSTON. "What good can your refusal do now?''

MRS. FRAZER. (*To Roylston*) "Your wife has plainly told me that she is firmly convinced I am your mistress. She has read letters to you from someone and thinks I am the author. You see how plainly impossible it would be for me to work for you or accept your assistance in any way. Besides, there are other reasons. I have made a mistake, a great mistake, and it only remains for me to go. Before I leave I should like to have you try to convince Mrs. Roylston that her suspicions are ground-less - as far as I am concerned.''

ROYLSTON. (*Turning to his wife*) "So you read my letters?''

MRS. ROYLSTON. "Yes; you left them on your table and I - couldn't resist the temptation.'' (*Roylston turns away from her contemptuously*) "I saw I was losing you, that you were be-coming indifferent to me and the children -''

ROYLSTON. "And you thought opening my letters would cure that?''

MRS. ROYLSTON. "They were already open.''

ROYLSTON. "Reading them, then.''

MRS. ROYLSTON. "I did not stop to think. I love you.''

ROYLSTON. (*Coldly*) "Indeed? You have strange ways of showing it.''

MRS. ROYLSTON. "I wanted to fight for you. I had to know who my enemy was.''

ROYLSTON. "Well, who was this so-called enemy of yours?''

MRS. ROYLSTON. "The letters were signed: Julia Wainright."

MRS. FRAZER. (*Eagerly*) "You see!"

ROYLSTON. "What has she to do with Mrs. Frazer? Why, in heaven's name, should you connect the two? Your insults to Mrs. Frazer are unpardonable and nonsensical. You are letting a narrow-minded suspicion blot out all that is best in you. Appearances have been against me before and yet you never took this attitude."

MRS. ROYLSTON. "There is such a thing as the last straw."

ROYLSTON. (*Sternly*) "Alice, what has come over you? You are not yourself. When I tell you we are both blameless do you still persist -"

MRS. ROYLSTON. (*Frenziedly*) "I don't believe you or her or anyone. I can't, I can't! You call her Mrs. Frazer and expect me to believe her innocent - and she wears no wedding ring." (*Mrs. Frazer instinctively hides her hand behind her back*) "Why are you up and out so early? You never get up before ten - Because she is up!"

MRS. FRAZER. (*Growing crimson*) "Oh!" (*The doorbell is heard ringing.*)

ROYLSTON. (*Bitingly*) "You need not tell your woes to the servants, Alice. Please try to control yourself. Here comes Benton." (*A moment later Benton appears in the doorway.*)

BENTON. "Dr. Morse is here, ma'am."

MRS. ROYLSTON. (*Faintly*) "Very well, Benton. Tell him I'll be right out; and call the children in."

BENTON. "Dr. Morse is here, ma'am."

ROYLSTON. (*Turning to his wife - cuttingly*) "Your conduct has been rather a revelation to me."

MRS. ROYLSTON. (*Wincing*) "Don't, David!"

ROYLSTON. "You have called me a liar and you have insulted Mrs. Frazer who is my friend." (*Mrs. Frazer makes an angry gesture repudiating this statement*) "You will have no cause for any suspicions in the future for I shall not trouble you with my presence in this house any longer. I will have Benton pack up my things at once. I do not care to live with a wife who is also an evil-minded spy. I could vindicate myself beyond all possibility of doubt, in ten words; but I prefer to have you think whatever your jealous whim dictates. I will explain to Mrs. Frazer and she may tell you if she considers your charges against her worth the trouble of refuting."

MRS. ROYLSTON. (*Shrinking from him as if he had struck her*) "Don't, don't David! Please don't speak like that - to me. You are killing me. I love you, you must not go away. This is your home. It is I who have no reason here. I will give you" (*Sobbing and walking toward the door on the left*) "your freedom. I want you to be happy, and - I know I'm only in your way - now. Please forgive me if I can't believe" (*Stretching out her arms to him supplicatingly*) "Please forgive me!" (*He turns away from her coldly.*)

MRS. FRAZER. (*Indignantly*) "For shame, Mr. Roylston!"

MRS. ROYLSTON. (*Turning to her furiously*) "How dare you intercede for me! Don't you know how I hate you?" (*She rushes out the door to the left as*

THE CURTAIN FALLS

"SERVITUDE" - ACT III

ACT III. The same - No time elapses between Acts 2 and 3. One is a continuation of the other.

SCENE: *The same. Roylston and Mrs. Frazer are still staring at the door through which Mrs. Roylston has just gone.*

ROYLSTON. (*Shrugging his shoulders turns to Mrs. F. with a short laugh*) "I have lived with that woman for eleven years, and have never known her until ten minutes ago." (*Benton appears in the doorway to the left. He stands there irresolutely for a second and is turning to go out again when Roylston sees him.*)

ROYLSTON. (*Sharply*) "Well, Benton? What is it?"

BENTON. (*Confused*) "Nothing of any importance, sir - just something the gardener, Weson, asked me to tell you." (*He hesitates, plainly indicating he does not wish to speak before Mrs. F.*)

ROYLSTON. (*To Mrs. Frazer*) "Excuse me." (*Goes over to Benton in the doorway*) "Well?"

BENTON. "Weson says he saw a suspicious character hanging around and looking at the house early this morning. Weson shouted at him to find out what he wanted and he ran away."

ROYLSTON. (*With a groan*) "Damn Weson! Are you never going to get over your idiotic burglar scares, Benton?"

BENTON. (*Darkly*) "I wasn't thinking of burglars - this time." (*With a meaning glance in Mrs. F.'s direction*) "Look out for the badger game, sir."

ROYLSTON. (*Irritably*) "Go to the devil!" (*Benton smiles craftily and goes out. Roylston comes back to the table*) "When I outgrew a governess they gave me Benton. I thought it was a change for the better but it wasn't. I have never been able to outgrow him. He won't let me." (*Mrs. Frazer remains silent. Roylston strides up and down nervously, clasping and unclasp-*

ing his hands and scowling at his disagreeable thoughts. Suddenly he strikes his fist into the palm of his hand with an impatient exclamation) "What a blind fool I am! If there was anything in the world I would have trusted Alice not to do, it was to read my letters. What a contemptible thing to do - to read my letters! And what a trustful simpleton I was to leave them around!" (*With an ironical smile*) "Do you remember what I said last night about not caring to analyze my home relations provided the surface remained smooth? Well, your visit has stirred up the depths with a vengeance - the muddy depths."

MRS. FRAZER. (*Sarcastically*) "What a crushing blow for you!"

ROYLSTON. "In all seriousness it really is appalling. I feel as if the world were turned topsy-turvy. When you have taken a thing for granted for years, when a faith in it has been one of the main props of your life, although you might not have realized its importance at the time, - and suddenly you make the discovery that you have trusted in a sham, that your prop is worm-eaten! - It is rather a rough tumble, isn't it?"

MRS. FRAZER. (*In the same sarcastic tone*) "I have found it so myself."

ROYLSTON. "That's so; I was forgetting. We're in the same boat, aren't we?" (*With a sigh*) "Well, I shall get bravely over it, as you have escaped from yours. A few bruises, I suppose, must be expected after such a hard fall."

MRS. FRAZER. "Yes, bruises on the soul."

ROYLSTON. "I will have to hunt a new illusion. You remember you said last night that when you came here you feared the crowning disillusionment?"

MRS. FRAZER. "My fears were well grounded."

ROYLSTON. "Hm - you mean you have seen my illusion go up in smoke, too? It is discouraging - as if everything in life were founded upon false appearances." (*He quotes ironically*) " 'Yea, faileth now dream the dreamer and the lute the lutanist'."

MRS. FRAZER. "You are deceiving yourself as to the nature of my awakening. I have come to regard the prop, as you call it, which I cast aside with scorn as the sound one. The new one, I find, is worm-eaten."

ROYLSTON. "The new one? Meaning that I am?"

MRS. FRAZER. "Exactly! I asked you to guide my future because I thought you were far-sighted. I have discovered you are only in-sighted - as pitifully in-sighted as I was."

ROYLSTON. (*Surprised*) "In-sighted?"

MRS. FRAZER. "Yes, you see nothing beyond yourself. You are so preoccupied with the workings of your own brain that your vision of outside things is clouded. You are only a cruel egotist."

ROYLSTON. "Know thyself, sayeth the law."

MRS. FRAZER. "You make no allowance for the individual."

ROYLSTON. "Oh, come now, Mrs. Frazer; you have read what I have written. You know if there is one thing I harp on ad nauseam -"

MRS. FRAZER. "It is the duty of the individual to triumph over environment; but in your life you regard yourself as the only individual in the world. You cannot see beyond that. You have reconstructed the world for yourself - well and good. Why try to force your conception on others? Why judge their thoughts by what you would think in their place? When you do so you deprive them of personality. You make them manikins and yourself the master of the show; and you care not a whit how you hurt their feelings when they fail to answer your pull of the string.''

ROYLSTON. (*With a bitter smile*) "You, too? It seems this is my day to be properly humbled in spirit."

MRS. FRAZER. "I know you will never pardon my effrontery in wounding your vanity so. Such colossal conceit!"

ROYLSTON. (*Flushing*) "Mrs. Frazer!"

MRS. FRAZER. (*Calmly*) "Your cruel vanity has torn off the mask. How could *you* help me? You can only help yourself. Perhaps if I were in love with you - but then you know, Mr. Narcissus, I would only be your reflection. However, I do not love you. Last night I thought - you were on such a high pedestal - I thought of the superman, of the creator, the maker of new values. This morning I saw merely an egotist whose hands are bloody with the human sacrifices he has made - to himself!"

ROYLSTON. (*Jumping from his chair - excitedly*) "You are unjust, Mrs. Frazer."

MRS. FRAZER. "Now you are begining to be angry."

ROYLSTON. (*Indignantly*) "Angry? Why should I be? You have a perfect right to your opinion, preposterous as it may be. Go on, let me hear the tale of my iniquities. It is very interesting."

MRS. FRAZER. (*Teasingly*) "You are losing your temper, you spoiled child."

ROYLSTON. "I am not losing my temper." (*Pettishly*) "I am growing inured to insults this morning."

MRS. FRAZER. "Why, so am I! I must beg your forgiveness for one thing I said. It was too cruel of me." (*She pauses, smiling mischievously at him.*)

ROYLSTON. (*Sulkily*) "To what are you alluding?"

MRS. FRAZER. (*Mockingly*) "I was truthful enough to tell you I did not love you. That was horrible of me. How could you endure hearing a woman say she did not love you? And how bored you must be when you hear them say they do love you! Eternal repetition, you know. The petted favorite of fortune stands between the devil and the deep blue sea."

ROYLSTON. (*Angrily*) "Mrs. Frazer, these personalities are -" (*Looking at her and catching the twinkle in her eyes - with an embarrassed laugh*) "I'm beaten; I acknowledge defeat. I surrender to the superwoman - only don't hit me when I'm down."

MRS. FRAZER. (*Contritely*) "I shouldn't have said all this to you, but I had to cure myself of my attack of hero-worship in some way. Besides the wounds I received in this morning's interview with your wife cried aloud for vengeance. I had to vent my spleen on someone."

ROYLSTON. (*Bitterly*) "I shall never forgive myself for subjecting you to such a breach of hospitality. It was shameful of her."

MRS. FRAZER. (*Sternly*) "No, it is shameful of you to speak of her in that way. She is not to blame for her suspicions. She loves you; how could she help thinking what she did? She is the most wonderful woman I have ever known - worlds above poor blind selfish creatures like you and me."

ROYLSTON. "I am afraid I cannot see it in that light."

MRS. FRAZER. "No, because in this case truth offends your pride and you will not see. You never misunderstood her as grossly as you do at the present moment."

ROYLSTON. "And *I* think I have only just begun to understand her."

MRS. FRAZER. "Take care! You are doing exactly what you rail against in others - judging by appearances. Is the keen analytical eye obstinately closed by wounded vanity?"

ROYLSTON. (*Impatiently*) "No, no - but my letters?"

MRS. FRAZER. "With such a wife you had no right to receive such letters."

ROYLSTON. (*Scornfully*) "Right?"

MRS. FRAZER. "You'll admit that needless cruelty is wrong, I hope?"

ROYLSTON. "Yes, but I don't see what -"

MRS. FRAZER. "Do you love this woman of the letters?"

ROYLSTON. "No, of course not!"

MRS. FRAZER. "Yet you persuaded her to leave her home -"

ROYLSTON. "Persuaded? No, certainly not! She came to me for advice. She had been impressed by what I had written about the narrowing influence of the conventional home. She had practically the same environment you described to me as yours before your marriage. She was engaged to be married to some cut-and-dried young simpleton. Her life was unsatisfying, gave her no scope for realizing the best that was in her. I saw she had brains, ability. I advised her to learn some occupation which would make her self-sustaining, and then go out into life and see things for herself."

MRS. FRAZER. "She is young?"

ROYLSTON. "Twenty-one."

MRS. FRAZER. "And pretty?"

ROYLSTON. "Yes."

MRS. FRAZER. "You are sure you are not in love with her?"

ROYLSTON. (*Irritably*) "I am sure, yes!" (*With a bored smile*) "I have been too busy to love anyone."

MRS. FRAZER. "But yourself. Then you have not even that justification."

ROYLSTON. (*Coldly*) "I see no necessity for justifying my actions."

MRS. FRAZER. "You cannot deny this girl loves you?"

ROYLSTON. (*Cynically*) "She may think she does."

MRS. FRAZER. "And you think she does! It tickles your vanity to think so."

ROYLSTON. "You are breaking me on the wheel." (*He laughs helplessly.*)

MRS. FRAZER. "You are a poor blind bat, not a butterfly; you can stand it. It may open your eyes. Can't you see that you have forever ruined all chance of her being happy with her cut-and-dried simpleton or any of his kind? And where is she to find the superman? Even if she gained your love, what a disappointment! What an awakening when she really came to know you!"

ROYLSTON. (*Forcing a laugh and looking down at his feet*) "Poor clay feet!"

MRS. FRAZER. "There is only one salvation for her. You must write to her at once and say -" (*She hesitates.*)

ROYLSTON. "Say what?"

MRS. FRAZER. "Reveal your true self."

ROYLSTON. (*Smiling confidently*) "You guarantee that will cure the infatuation?"

MRS. FRAZER. "Absolutely!"

ROYLSTON. "Are you sure she won't read her ideal into my words?"

MRS. FRAZER. (*Biting her lip*) "Perhaps you are right. That wont't do. I must go to her and tell her -"

ROYLSTON. "She would think you were jealous. She would not believe you."

MRS. FRAZER. "Tell her flatly you don't love her."

ROYLSTON. "How about needless cruelty?"

MRS. FRAZER. (*Alarmed*) "But you see yourself you must end it someway."

ROYLSTON. "I have a way" (*Smiling at her*) "tried and proved by experience."

MRS. FRAZER. (*Scornfully*) "I have no doubt."

ROYLSTON. (*In a bantering tone*) "Shall I tell you what it is? Don't try to look so indifferent. You know you're dying with curiosity." (*Mrs. Frazer shakes her head indignantly*) "Well, I write a letter to this effect: 'I love you but we must see each other no more'."

MRS. FRAZER. (*Contemptuously*) "Oh!"

ROYLSTON. (*Continues with a great show of affected pathos*) "I cannot make you unhappy. Our love is forbidden by cruel, man-made laws and it is on your frail shoulders their punishment would fall, etc., ad nauseam. So you must forget me - or rather, do not forget. Remember in my heart of hearts, my soul of souls, etc., ad lib, your image will remain, the inspiration of my work; that in spirit all my work will be dedicated to you - and so on ad infinitum."

MRS. FRAZER. "That is disgusting drivel."

ROYLSTON. "Of course it is! But don't you know, haven't you ever been in love?"

MRS. FRAZER. "Why?"

ROYLSTON. "Love is the world upside down. Sense is drivel and drivel is sense."

MRS. FRAZER. "You mean to tell me she will be ridiculous enough to believe that?"

ROYLSTON. "She will revel in it. She will telephone - I cannot be found. She will write - no answer. She may even try to see me - I am invisible. Then she will say: That wonderful man has the strength to sacrifice himself for my sake. Voila! She goes home, marries the cut-and-dried simpleton, adopts a superior air which holds him in awed servitude, pities him - pity is love without jealousy - and whenever his uncouth matter-of-factness grates on her sensitive nerves she reverently takes my image from the inner shrine and indulges in the sweet happiness of melancholy retrospection. The memory of another's sacrifice for love of oneself - That is the most soothing narcotic a woman can possess. I recommend it to you."

MRS. FRAZER. (*Dryly*) "Thank you."

ROYLSTON. (*Enthusiastically*) "Just think of the ecstatic joy of a woman grown old and fat when she remembers that in her younger days a discarded lover committed suicide because she refused him. What a recompense for a double chin the memory of such a corpse must be!"

MRS. FRAZER. (*Controlling an impulse to laugh - coldly*) "I was attempting to consider this matter seriously."

ROYLSTON. "What! Consider love seriously? Set your mind at rest. I have written the letter and I have ordered Benton to stifle the appeals of the telephone. You see you need not have warned me."

MRS. FRAZER. "She had become serious, then?"

ROYLSTON. "Why do you say that?"

MRS. FRAZER. "When they become serious you grow afraid of complications. A little bird told me."

ROYLSTON. "A little bird?"

MRS. FRAZER. "A man is never a hero to his -"

ROYLSTON. (*Groaning*) "Valet! That scoundrel Benton! The model of discretion. Another illusion gone! My house of cards is tumbling about my ears."

MRS. FRAZER. "No more than you deserve."

ROYLSTON. "I admit it, Mrs. Frazer" (*Eagerly*) "I may mock but I see it just the same. In the future I will send my tickled vanity a-packing and have done with such foolishness. After all, it was only an amusing flirtation - nothing more."

MRS. FRAZER. "Go and tell Mrs. Roylston that."

ROYLSTON. (*His expression growing hard and cold*) "Thank you for reminding me." (*He goes to the electric bell-button in the wall near the door on left.*)

MRS. FRAZER. (*Anxiously*) "What are you going to do?"

ROYLSTON. "Ring for Benton to pack my things."

MRS. FRAZER. "Please don't!"

ROYLSTON. "Why not?"

MRS. FRAZER. (*Pleadingly*) "Not yet at any rate. Please sit down again. I have something to say to you."

ROYLSTON. (*Sitting down*) "Whatever you may say, Mrs. Frazer, will not alter my opinion in the least. I have my own ideas of the way Alice has acted and what I must do. With your permission I will go back to New York on the train with you."

MRS. FRAZER. "No, no, no! Think of how that would hurt her? Have you no pity? I will not allow it. Furthermore you will never see me again when I leave this house. I have been the cause of too much unhappiness already."

ROYLSTON. "Don't accuse yourself. I have only gratitude to you for opening my eyes, and I want to help you in every way as I promised I would."

MRS. FRAZER. (*Vehemently*) "No!"

ROYLSTON. "Surely you don't mean you refuse -"

MRS. FRAZER. "Yes, I refuse your assistance in any way, shape or manner. I am not going to take any position and I will not need your help; so let us drop that part of the matter. And as for opening your eyes you have never been as sightless as you are now, poor blind mole!"

ROYLSTON. (*With smiling protest*) "Odious comparisons! First I am a bat, then a mole!"

MRS. FRAZER. "Would you like to see clearly?"

ROYLSTON. "Granted that I am blind - will sight make me any the less miserable?"

MRS. FRAZER (*Enthusiastically*) "It will make you happy, truly happy." (*R. smiles skeptically*) "Have I your permission to teach you the lesson I was given this morning."

ROYLSTON. (*Frowning*) "Lesson?"

MRS. FRAZER. "Yes, a lesson in life your wife gave me this morning."

ROYLSTON. (*Icily*) "My wife also gave me a lesson in life, if you will remember" (*Dryly*) "Her first lesson was not so pleasing that I crave for a second."

MRS. FRAZER. "For her sake, for my sake, for your own sake you must."

ROYLSTON. (*Indifferently*) "Very well." (*He gets up from his chair*) " In the meantime Benton can be packing up my things."

MRS. FRAZER. "No, please, not yet. Hear me out first - then pack away if you still care to." (*He hesitates uncertainly*) "Come, I ask it as a favor." (*He sits down in his chair again.*)

ROYLSTON. "I warn you, Mrs. Frazer, I am not to be cajoled into altering my plans. You are wasting your time and eloquence."

MRS. FRAZER. "We shall see. Remember you are to hear me from begining to end - of the lesson. All ready? When I came down this morning I found the irreproachable Benton in this room."

ROYLSTON. "And he showed you the crack in my armor."

MRS. FRAZER. "He convinced me, without meaning to do so, that the idol's feet were - well - at least only plated."

ROYLSTON. (*Sarcastically*) "Of course, he meant well."

MRS. FRAZER. "He meant to flatter me. He had his own convictions as to my status in this household, and when I saw him growing confidential I did not attempt to show him his mistake."

ROYLSTON. (*Accusingly*) "You wanted to listen to his gossip?"

MRS. FRAZER. (*With a frank laugh*) "I wanted to play detective and find out if my you was the real you. Benton, having approved of your choice of a mistress, flattered me by revealing the fact that you had never cared enough for any of the others to dare to install them in your household."

ROYLSTON. (*Raging*) "The evil-minded wretch! Others, indeed! I tell you that there never have been any others in the sense he meant. And you allowed him to talk to you like that?"

MRS. FRAZER. "I was making an ineffectual attempt to put him in his place when we heard Mrs. Roylston coming in with the children. And what do you think I did? - I, the bold emancipated woman? I ran and hid in that room like the guiltiest of cravens. When I regained control of myself I was furious, and to prove I was not a coward I came in to face your wife.

I went to the other extreme in my display of daring. She was not certain I had been here all night but I immediately told her the truth of the whole affair."

ROYLSTON. "What else could you have done?"

MRS. FRAZER. "Oh, I could have lied a little for the good of her soul. Just consider how damning the facts are! She returns unexpectedly to find me sneaking out of a darkened room, the picture of guilt. I brazenly acknowledge I have been here all night and tell her an absurd story of missing a train, and so forth. She has read letters and -"

ROYLSTON. (*Impatiently*) "I know how sadly the circumstantial evidence is against the truth. I was relying on the implicit trust she has always seemed to have for me."

MRS. FRAZER. "Trust? After she had read those letters - letters which seemed all the more guilty because you had never mentioned them to her? Trust! You want an angel for a wife, not a human being."

ROYLSTON. "She had no business to read those letters. The whole thing rests upon that."

MRS. FRAZER. "You had no business to receive the letters. The whole thing rests upon that. But to go on with my lesson: I asserted my innocence. Your wife refused to believe me - naturally enough. She spoke despondently of having expected something of the sort for a long time because you had been growing indifferent to her and the children."

ROYLSTON. (*Indignantly*) "That is not so. It's true I haven't had much time. I have been very busy, but -"

MRS. FRAZER. (*Looking at him searchingly*) "Are you sure what you are saying now is the truth. Come, be frank! Remember your statement to me last night when I asked you if you loved her."

ROYLSTON. (*After a pause - grudgingly*) "Well, I confess I may have seemed indifferent; but, good heavens -"

MRS. FRAZER. "She said she blamed no one but herself for what had happened. How could it be expected that a brilliant genius like you could continue to love a poor ignorant creature like herself?"

ROYLSTON. (*A bit shamefaced*) "She said that?"

MRS. FRAZER. "Those are almost her exact words. She blamed herself for marrying you in the first place. Marriages like yours were cursed, she thought."

ROYLSTON. "Marriages like ours?"

MRS. FRAZER. (*Meaningly - looking steadily into his eyes*) "She told me of the events which preceded your marriage - of the discovery of your love affair."

ROYLSTON. (*Gripping the arms of his chair tensely, and speaking hoarsely*) "Good God, she told you that! Poor Alice!" (*Half to himself*) "What could have made her do that?"

MRS. FRAZER. "She said she thought that perhaps you blamed her for your father's death."

ROYLSTON. "What an absurd idea!"

MRS. FRAZER. "She described your early life together - the days of struggle with poverty before your first play was produced; the days when you remained home in the little flat to write while she worked in an office as stenographer. She used to typewrite what you had written during the day when she came home at night - after she had cooked dinner and washed the dishes."

ROYLSTON. (*His face slowly flushing crimson*) "You are right! I see what you are driving at. Whatever I am she has made me. I have been forgetting those early days for the past

few years. They do not chime well with the tickled vanity."
(*With sudden ingenuousness*) "But I did used to dry the dishes,
you know."

MRS. FRAZER. (*Laughing*) "Bravo! Richard is himself again.
You only sold a few articles that first year, she said."

ROYLSTON. "She flattered me. I never sold one. Every cent
came through her."

MRS. FRAZER. "She said those days were the happiest of her
life. She had often been selfish enough to wish, since you became
indifferent, that you had never succeeded and it could always
have been as it was in the little flat."

ROYLSTON. "Good heavens, she was nothing but a slave in
those days."

MRS. FRAZER. "She knew how hard it must have been for
you, who had been used to having everything, to have her drag
you down into privation and -"

ROYLSTON. (*Deeply moved*) "What a horribly mistaken
thought! I joyed in losing everything for her. It was like paying
off part of my debt."

MRS. FRAZER. (*Continuing as if he had not interrupted*) "So
she resolved that as soon as your first book or play was published
or produced, and you did not need her any longer, she would
leave you, permit you to regain your freedom."

ROYLSTON. (*Stupefied - his voice trembling*) "Why that's
what she proposed to do - for me - when she was here a little
while ago!"

MRS. FRAZER. "Oh yes, she only desires your happiness and,
as she thinks you love me, she is perfectly willing to give you
up to me - because she loves you so much."

ROYLSTON. "How is it possible to lose oneself like that - I

cannot grasp it - there is too much clay in my make-up - For me, too! Good heavens! She intended to leave me when my first play was produced, you say? But she didn't."

MRS. FRAZER. "For a very good reason. It was about that time your son was born, wasn't it?"

ROYLSTON. (*Getting up from his chair and walking nervously about the room - in great agitation*) "I see, I see! Poor Alice! What a woman she is! And I - good heavens! You threatened to open my eyes - I've lived with her all these years and forgotten how much I owed to her. She has protected and shielded me from everything - made my opportunity for me, you might say - and I took it all for granted - the finest thing in my life! Took it all for granted without a thought of gratitude, as my due. Lord, what a cad I've been! What a rotten cad!" (*He throws himself into the chair and stares moodily before him.*)

MRS. FRAZER. (*With a faint smile*) "I'd like to deny your statement but I'm afraid it's only too true."

ROYLSTON. "What I cannot get through my head is why she should tell you all this. Alice is proud. To reveal all this to you, a stranger - it must have humbled her spirit to the breaking point."

MRS. FRAZER. "I cannot quite understand, myself. She wished to justify you, of course, to prove you were in no way to blame."

ROYLSTON. (*Groaning*) "Oh!"

MRS. FRAZER. "You see she persisted in regarding this misfortune as the retribution for her sin in the beginning."

ROYLSTON. (*Jumping up - excitedly*) "Ah, by heavens, that is going too far! Retribution for *her* sin! What a preposterous idea! As if the blame, the sin if it was one, were not all mine!" (*Looking at his hands*) "Bloody with sacrifices at my own altar - yes, you were right - and she is the woman whom I tortured with my blind egotism not half an hour ago - the woman who pleaded for forgiveness - and I refused and was going to desert her. I am beginning to hate myself for a monster! Those letters! If any woman ever dares to write to me again I'll have her letters burned by the - no, we haven't one - I'll hand them over to the police." (*Mrs. Frazer bursts out laughing*) "And my children - Good God, do you know the horrible thought came to me just now that I do not even know my own children?"

MRS. FRAZER. (*Protestingly*) "Now you are carrying your self-accusation too far."

ROYLSTON. (*Vehemently*) "I tell you it's the truth. I speak to them, I kiss them sometimes; but I do the same for other people's. For all the loving interest I have taken in them they might just as well be the gardener's - or Benton's."

MRS. FRAZER. "You have the whole future before you for retribution."

ROYLSTON. (*Catching at the word eagerly*) "Yes, retribution, joyful retribution every day, every hour! Pay off a part of this enormous debt of love which has accumulated against me! Why, life is going to mean more, be finer and happier than I ever dreamed!"

MRS. FRAZER. "Happiness is servitude."

ROYLSTON. (*Enthusiastically*) "Of course it is! Servitude in love, love in servitude! Logos in Pan, Pan in Logos! That is the great secret - and I never knew! Thank you, thank you! But how did you guess it?"

MRS. FRAZER. "Mrs. Roylston told me this morning - her lesson in life."

ROYLSTON. "That, too! Her love is great enough to solve all enigmas."

MRS. FRAZER. (*Laughing*) But your work? The sovereign individual? The superman? The great lonely one?"

ROYLSTON. "My love will be a superlove worthy of the superman, and - " (*Hesitating*) "Besides this is the exceptional case which proves the contrary rule - what are you laughing at?"

MRS. FRAZER. "At your determination to be exceptional though the heavens fall."

ROYLSTON. (*Laughing himself*) "I have to be exceptional to be worthy of such an exceptional wife."

MRS. FRAZER. (*Rising from her chair*) "And now I must go. My mission is accomplished."

ROYLSTON. "Your mission?" (*The doorbell is heard ringing.*)

MRS. FRAZER. "Remember what you said about fatality? I am convinced I had to accomplish something here. It was not what I thought it was, but no matter. I, too, have learned the secret. It was my mission to open your eyes - and my own."

ROYLSTON. "You are going back to your husband?"

MRS. FRAZER. "Yes, back to the chains which have suddenly become dear to me. Like you I had grown so accustomed to the best things in life that I scorned it. I, too, have my joyful retribution to make, my debt of love to pay."

ROYLSTON. (*Going to her and taking her hand*) "And how can I ever thank you for my awakening?"

MRS. FRAZER. "The fact that you have wakened is thanks enough."

ROYLSTON. "And will you not become - my wife's friend?"

MRS. FRAZER. "With all my heart - if she will allow it."

(*Benton appears in the doorway on the left. He is greatly excited.*)

BENTON. "Excuse me, sir, but there's a man who insisted on seeing you and -'" (*George Frazer pushes Benton roughly aside and steps into the room. He is a man of about thirty-five, thick-set, of medium height, black hair grey at the temples, square jaw, irregular features, broad clean-shaven face, and shrewd blue eyes. His face is haggard and shows plainly the traces of deep-rooted grief and anxiety with their consequent sleepless nights. He is dressed in a business suit of dark material.*)

FRAZER. (*Gives a groan of suppressed rage as he sees the two standing together*) "Ethel!"

MRS. FRAZER. "George!" (*She makes a movement toward him. He throws himself at Roylston, pulling a revolver from his coat pocket. Mrs. Frazer springs between them.*)

MRS. FRAZER. "For my sake! George!" (*Frazer hurls the revolver on the floor and sinks into the chair by the table, hiding his face in his hands and sobbing heavily. Mrs. Frazer goes to him and puts her arm around his shoulder. He makes a feeble effort to shake her off. Benton creeps stealthily over and picks up the revolver.*)

ROYLSTON. (*Severely*) "You may go, Benton." (*Benton looks at him irresolutely, then goes out. Frazer finally regains his composure somewhat and turns his grief-stricken face to his wife.*)

FRAZER. "Ethel - why? - My God!"

MRS. FRAZER. (*Distractedly*) "Will this misunderstanding never be cleared up!"

ROYLSTON. "Yes, I will clear it up."

FRAZER. (*Furiously*) "Shut up, you - . You lie! I know what I know. You have done me harm enough without trying to treat me like a fool. I'd have shot you for the skulking liar you are - but - it wasn't for your sake I didn't -"

ROYLSTON. (*With calm dignity*) "I choose to ignore your insults for the present, Mr. Frazer. When you are calmer you will hear what I have to say and this ludicrous melodrama will end." (*He turns to go out door in back.*)

MRS. FRAZER. "No, please stay; you must." (*R. remains standing by the door.*)

MRS. FRAZER. (*Her voice trembling*) "George, how did you find out?"

FRAZER. "I always knew you'd wind up here sooner or later. Before you left, when I was certain you didn't care for me any more, I suspected you were in love with this" (*With bitter scorn*) "gentleman. His books, his plays all over the place, his photograph on the middle of your dresser" (*Mrs. Frazer flushes. Roylston looks at her in astonishment*) "That was why I had you followed."

MRS. FRAZER. (*With a frown*) "I thought you had given up spying on me."

FRAZER. (*Pleadingly*) "It wasn't spying. You musn't think that, Ethel. It was for your own sake I did it."

MRS. FRAZER. (*With a hard laugh*) "For my sake!"

FRAZER. "I wanted to protect you. You don't know the world. I knew you'd do something foolish sooner or later with your head full of his crazy ideas. You don't know the game these gentlemen play."

ROYLSTON. (*Angrily*) "Oh!" (*He turns and goes out door in rear.*)

MRS. FRAZER. "So I was followed to this house?"

FRAZER. "Yes."

MRS. FRAZER. "When I came - last night?"

FRAZER. (*With a groan*) "Yes."

MRS. FRAZER. "How is it you gave up waiting for me? Why haven't you tried to see me yourself - it's nearly two months."

FRAZER. "I could see you didn't want me bothering you - and I've been sick."

MRS. FRAZER. (*Alarmed*) "Sick?"

FRAZER. (*Lightly*) "Nothing serious - overwork - nervous breakdown, the doctor said. Had to go to bed - he prescribed perfect rest" (*Ironically*) "Perfect rest!"

˙ MRS. FRAZER. (*With tender anxiety*) "But you're all right now, de - " (*She bites back the term of endearment at his wondering look*) "George?"

FRAZER. (*Sarcastically*) "Fine - as you can see."

MRS. FRAZER. "Why couldn't you have sent me word? It would have changed things so."

FRAZER. "You mean you wouldn't be here? Well, I couldn't. I didn't want you to come back because you pitied me." (*Bitterly*) "I didn't think you'd care."

MRS. FRAZER. (*Wincing*) "Oh" (*After a pause*) "Why did you come here this morning?"

FRAZER. "The detective telephoned me - when he was sure. I wanted to kill this man and you too, at first. I didn't know what I was doing."

MRS. FRAZER. (*Sadly*) "And now I suppose it's all over - forever - between us. You can't want me any longer - believing what you do."

FRAZER. (*Turning away from her to hide his emotion*) Don't say that, Ethel. I can't give you up - this way. Life is too

- hard to bear - without you. I can't help loving you - in spite
of everything. I shouldn't - I suppose - now" (*Mrs. Frazer is
looking at him with eyes full of tenderness*) "If you'd only -
love me a little - I could forget this foolishness - not your fault
- if we'd had children - you were always alone - my fault." (*A
sob shakes his shoulders.*)

MRS. FRAZER. (*Softly*) "So you still want me - to come
back?"

FRAZER. "Yes - that's why I came - to ask you - if you
would."

MRS. FRAZER. (*Kneeling down beside him - eagerly*) "Then
look into my eyes quick - now!" (*He looks down at her*) "I
swear to you I am innocent - that I love you more now than
I ever did, even on our honeymoon; and I am as innocent of
wrong now as I was then. Can you believe me?"

FRAZER. (*Wonderingly*) "Then you don't love him?"

MRS. FRAZER. "No, no, a thousand times no! I love you, and
he loves his wife. My presence here is folly, nothing more. Let
me explain the whole thing to you."

FRAZER. (*Joyfully*) "No, no, I believe you without that."
(*He takes her into his arms and kisses her*) Mrs. Roylston
enters from the door on the left. She has a small travelling bag
in her hand. Her eyes are red from weeping. She stops in astonishment and her bag drops from her hand when she sees the
Frazers.*)

MRS. ROYLSTON. (*Timidly*) "I beg your pardon." (*Startled,
they both jump to their feet and face Mrs. Roylston in confusion.*)

MRS. FRAZER. (*Joyfully*) " I want you to meet my husband,
Mrs. Roylston. George, this is Mrs. Roylston."

MRS. ROYLSTON. (*Astonished*) "I'm very happy -"

FRAZER. "A great pleasure, etc."

MRS. FRAZER. "Mrs. Roylston is the most wonderful woman in the world." (*Mrs. Roylston smiles feebly*) "If you don't believe me, ask her husband." (*As Frazer stammers and Mrs. Roylston is equally nonplussed*) "And now you and I will be going - home!" (*She walks over toward the door on the left*) "Good-bye, Mrs. Roylston. I hope when you understand everything you will become my friend." (*She holds out her hand which Mrs. Roylston takes uncertainly as if in a daze*) "Come, George, out into the open air. I have so much to say to you." (*She goes out. Frazer follows her but stops at the door and turns to Mrs. Roylston.*)

FRAZER. "Mrs. Roylston, will you tell your husband I wish to take back all I said to him a while ago. He'll understand."

MRS. ROYLSTON. (*Dully*) "I'll tell him."

FRAZER. "Thank you; good-bye." (*He goes out. A moment later the front door is heard closing.*)

MRS. ROYLSTON. (*Mechanically*) "Good-bye." (*She takes her bag and sets it down beside the table; then sinks wearily into the chair and leans both elbows on the table, holding her face in her hands in an attitude of deep dejection. Roylston enters from the door in the rear. He gives a joyful exclamation on seeing his wife.*)

ROYLSTON. (*Coming over quickly, stands beside her*) "Alice."

MRS. ROYLSTON. (*Startled, turns and looks up at him - dully*) "Yes."

ROYLSTON. "They have gone - Mr. and Mrs. Frazer - together?"

MRS. ROYLSTON. "Yes."

ROYLSTON. (*Jubilantly*) "Good! And without hearing my

explanation! That is a proof of love and trust on his part which I would hardly have expected of him. You see, Alice, the most ludicrous part of this whole misunderstanding is the fact that I did not spend last night in this house."

MRS. ROYLSTON. (*Slowly - as if she could not believe her ears*) "You - were not here?"

ROYLSTON. "No. After I directed Mrs. Frazer to her room I ran away - spent the night at the roadhouse. I was afraid to stay, I must confess - afraid of myself - afraid of how the situation might be misconstrued. I didn't want to be the cause of any more trouble to Mrs. Frazer, who had suffered enough already."

MRS. ROYLSTON. (*Her eyes brimming with happy tears*) "Oh, I'm so glad!"

ROYLSTON. "I want you to prove my statement - to be completely satisfied that I am speaking the truth. My name is on the register at the roadhouse and they all know me and can testify to my story. I wanted to explain before but your doubts hurt my obstinate pride - I had boasted to Mrs. Frazer that you would not judge by appearances, you know. As for Frazer's detective, he must have taken everything for granted - as you and all the rest did. I'll have to write to Frazer and tell him. In spite of his fine confidence there might be some secret suspicions in the back of his mind."

MRS. ROYLSTON. "David - forgive me -"

ROYLSTON. (*Impetuously*) "Forgive you? What nonsense!" (*He bends down to kneel beside her and knocks his knee against her bag. He holds it up wonderingly*) "What's this? Your bag all packed! Then you were really going to leave me?"

MRS. ROYLSTON. (*Tremblingly*) "I thought you loved her. I wanted you to be happy."

ROYLSTON. "And the children?"

MRS. ROYLSTON. "I had no right - It was best for them to stay."

ROYLSTON. "You were going to leave them, too - and all for my sake! Good heavens! And you ask for forgiveness!" (*Kneeling down beside her and putting his arms around her*) "Ah, my dear, my dear, how deeply you make me feel my unworthiness! I am the one who must plead for pardon, pardon for a lifetime of selfish neglect, of vain posing, of stupid conceit -"

MRS. ROYLSTON. (*Kissing him*) "Ssshhh!"

ROYLSTON. (*His voice vibrating with tenderness*) "Dear, the future will be all that the past has not been, I swear it. We start on our honeymoon today - a lifelong honeymoon." (*Jumping to his feet, with mock severity*) "But haven't you read your husband's books, you wonderful, foolish woman? Don't you know it was your duty to claim your right as an individual, to shake off the shackles my insufferable egotism had forced upon you? Don't you understand that you have stifled your own longings, given up your own happiness that I might feel self-satisfied -"

MRS. ROYLSTON. (*Interrupting him - softly and tenderly*) "That was my happiness." (*He bends down and kisses her reverently as*

THE CURTAIN FALLS

"A WIFE FOR A LIFE" (1913)

A Play In One Act

Cast of Characters

THE OLDER MAN

JACK, *The Younger Man.*

OLD PETE, *a miner.*

SCENE: *The edge of the Arizona desert; a plain dotted in the foreground with clumps of sagebrush. On the horizon a lonely butte is outlined, black and sinister against the lighter darkness of a sky with stars. The time is in the early hours of the night. In the foreground stands a ragged tent the flap of which is open. Leaning against it are some shovels and a pick or two. Two saddles are on the ground nearby. Before the tent is a smouldering camp fire at which an elderly man of about fifty is seated. He is dressed in miner's costume; flannel shirt, khaki trousers, high boots etc. - all patched and showing evidences of long wear and tear. His wide-brimmed Stetson hat lies on the ground beside him. His hair is turning gray and his face is the face of one who has wandered far, lived hard, seen life in the rough, and is a little weary of it all. Withal his air and speech are those of an educated man whose native refinement has clung to him in spite of many hard knocks.*

On one side of the tent stands a rough stool and a gold-miner's panning tub - a square box half filled with water.

THE OLDER MAN. (*stirring the fire in a futile attempt to start it into flame*) "I wonder what can be keeping him so long?" (*hears noise of someone approaching*) "Hello Jack, I was just beginning to think you were lost."

(*Old Pete enters. He is an old man dressed in rough miner's costume but he wears spurs and carries a quirt in his hand. He is covered with dust and has evidently been riding hard.*)

OLD PETE. "It aint Jack. It's me."

THE OLDER MAN. (*disappointed*) "Hello Pete. What brings you around at this time of the night?"

OLD PETE. (*taking telegram from his pocket*) "I was just leaving Lawson when the operator stopped me and give me this for Jack. I seen your camp fire burning and reckoned I'd bring it right over."

THE OLDER MAN. (*taking telegram*) "Many thanks Pete. Won't you sit down and rest a bit?"

OLD PETE. "Much obliged but I reckon I'll travel along. I ain't slept none to speak of in the past few nights and I got to be up at sunrise." (*grinning sheepishly*) "That fool town of Lawson sure does keep you up nights (*he starts to go, then stops*) "Claim panning out as good as ever?"

THE OLDER MAN. "Better every day. This morning we took a sample from the upper end which we haven't touched so far. It looks good but we haven't panned it yet."

OLD PETE. "You-alls ought to get rich. You know how to keep money. Now me and money never could get on noway (*pulls out pockets ruefully*) "They cleaned me out in Lawson this time and I reckon they'll clean me again the next time." (*shaking his head*) "Cities is sure hell that-a-way. Adios." (*Exits.*)

THE OLDER MAN. "Good night. Poor Pete. Same old story. Been bucking the faro bank again I suppose." (*looks at telegram*) "Hmm. Wonder what this is?" "Jack has had no correspondence in the five years I've been with him. May be something important in connection with the mine. I guess I'd better open it. He won't mind anyway." (*he opens the telegram and reads aloud*) " 'I am waiting. Come' No name signed. It comes from New York too. Well it's too many for me. I give it up." (*puts telegram in pocket*) "Must be that fool operator got mixed up in his names. I wouldn't like to see Jack obey any summons like that. He's about all I've got now and I'd hate to see him leave just when we've struck it rich." (*dismissing the subject*) "I guess this wire is all a mistake anyway." (*he looks around yawning and his eye lights on the panning tub*) "Now if only the upper part of the claim is as rich as that we've been working" - (*the noise of someone approaching is heard*) "Here he comes now. Welcome wanderer! Where have you been all this time?''

(*Jack enters. He is dressed about the same as the Older Man but is much younger - in the early thirties.*)

JACK. "One of the horses slipt his hobbles and I had quite a hunt for him. I finally found him down by the spring wallowing around as if water were the commonest thing in this section of Arizona. Fool beast!''

THE OLDER MAN. (*forgetting all about the telegram*) "It's a strange thing we should run into water out here where the maps say there isn't any. It's the one blessing we've found in this land God forgot. We're fools for luck for once.''

JACK. (*nodding*) "Yes" (*then rather exultantly*) "But we have small cause to kick about this lonely hole after all. Any place is God's country to a man if there's gold in it and he finds it. There's gold here and (*taking a small bag from his pocket and shaking it*) we've found it. So long live the desert say I.''

THE OLDER MAN. "Those are my sentiments.'' (*he rolls a cigarette paper and setting it afire in the flame lights his pipe*) "It sure looks as if our ship had come in at last here on the rim of the world. The luck was due to change. We've had our share of the bad variety; just missing a strike in every jumping-off place from South Africa to Alaska. We've taken our hard knocks with the imitation of a laugh at any rate and (*stretching out his hand to the younger man who grasps it heartily*) we've been good pals ever since that day in the Transvaal five years ago when you hauled me out of the river, saved my life, and our friendship began.'' (*as the younger man starts to speak*) "No you needn't try to stop me expressing my gratitude. I haven't forgotten that day and I never will.''

JACK. (*to change the subject*) "I'm going to see what that

prospect we took at the other end of the claim looks like." (*he goes into the tent and returns with a gold pan heaped with dirt under his arm and sitting down in front of the panning tub proceeds to test the prospect. He washes the heap of dirt down until there is but a handful of gravel left. The Older Man comes over and stands behind him looking over his shoulder. Finally after one quick flip of the pan Jack points to the sediment left in the bottom in which a small heap of bright yellow particles can be seen.*) "What do you think of that?"

THE OLDER MAN. (*reaching over and feeling them with his fingers*) "O'course gold; just as I expected. The upper end of the claim is just as rich as it is down here."

JACK. (*with growing excitement*) "There's over a quarter of an ounce here at least. That's five dollars a pan - better than we've ever panned down here at any time since we made the strike four months ago." (*lays the pan aside*) "I tell you this claim is too much for us to handle alone. One of us ought to go East and organize a company."

THE OLDER MAN. "Then it will have to be you. I'm too old" (*Jack smiles and makes a deprecating gesture*) "Anyway I never could get along with civilization and (*laughing*) civilization never cared overmuch for me." (*goes over and sits down by the fire*) - (*after a pause*) "You've seemed to be hankering after the East quite a lot in the last month or so." (*smiling*) "Getting tired of the company here eh?"

JACK. (*quickly*) "No you know that isn't so after all the years we've been pals and all we've been through together."

THE OLDER MAN. (*jokingly*) "Then what is the attraction the effete East has to offer? (*mockingly*) It's a woman I suppose?"

JACK. (*with dignity*) "An angel rather."

THE OLDER MAN. (*cynically*) "They're all angels - at first. The only trouble is their angelic attributes lack staying qualities (*then half bitterly*) At any rate you'd find them hard to prove by my experiences."

JACK. (*shrugging his shoulders a little impatiently*) "You're a disgusting cynic and I refuse to argue. You know we've never been able to agree on that subject. I'm going to hunt out that bottle we've carried about so long and we'll drink to the mine and future prosperity." (*he goes into tent*) "Here it is." (*He returns with a quart of whiskey, opens it with a knife and pours out two drinks in the tin cups.*) (*laughing*) "I think this is a proper occasion for celebration - the two Prodigals welcome the fatted calf. Let's make it a christening also. Here's to the Yvette mine!"

The Older Man who has been laughing turns suddenly grim. His hand trembles as he clinks cups and he almost spills some of the whiskey. He speaks in harsh jerky tones; "Why the Yvette?"

JACK. (*not noticing his agitation*) "I know it sounds like rather a frivolous name for a mine but I have a hunch. There's a romance back of it - my romance. That was her name. One rarely speaks of such things. I've never told you but I will now if you care to hear it. It was over a year before I met you. I had just been out of mining school a short time and was prospecting around in the mountains of Peru hoping to hit a bonanza there. At the time I speak of I had returned to reoutfit at a small mining camp near the frontier of Ecuador. It was there I met her. She was the wife of a broken-down mining engineer from the States, over twenty years her senior. (*the Older Man who has been listening intently is poking the fire nervously and his face becomes harsher and harsher*) "According to all accounts he was a drunken brute who left her alone most of the time and only lived from one drunk to another. Personally I never saw him. It was probably better that I did not. You see I fell in love with her on the spot and the thought of how he treated her made my blood boil."

THE OLDER MAN. (*in stifled tones*) "What was the name of the mining town you mention? I've been in that country myself - many years ago."

JACK. "San Sebastien. Do you know it?"

At the words "San Sebastien" the Older Man seems to crumple up. Nothing seems alive about him but his eyes, staring horribly, and his right hand which nervously fingers the gun in the belt around his waist.

THE OLDER MAN. (*in a hoarse whisper*) "Yes. I know it. Go on."

JACK. (*dreamily, absorbed in his own thoughts*) "I loved her. In the corrupt environment of a mining camp she seemed like a lily growing in a field of rank weeds. I longed to take her away from all that atmosphere of sordid sin and suffering; away from her beast of a husband who was steadily ruining that beautiful young life and driving her to desperation. I overstayed my time. I should have been back in the mountains. I went to see her often. He was always away it seemed. Finally people began to talk. Then I realized that the time had come and I told her that I loved her. I shall never forget her face. She looked at me with great calm eyes but her lips trembled as she said: 'I know you love me and I - I love you; but you must go away and we must never see each other again. I am his wife and I must keep my pledge'."

THE OLDER MAN. (*starting to his feet and half drawing the pistol from the holster*) "You lie!"

JACK. (*rudely awakened from his dream also springs to his feet, his face angry and perplexed*) "Why what do you mean? What is it?"

THE OLDER MAN. (*controlling his rage with a mighty effort and sitting down again*) "Nothing. Nerves I guess. It's my sore spot - the virtue of women. I've seen but little of it in my mining camp experiences and your heroine seems to me too impossible. (*wonderingly Jack sits down beside him again.*)

JACK. (*eagerly*) "You wouldn't think so if you could have seen her. (*the Older Man covers his face in his hands and groans.*) "Here's a picture of her she sent me a year ago." (*takes small photo out of pocket of his shirt*) "Look at it" (*handing him the photo*) "Do you think a woman with a face like that could be the regular mining camp kind?" (*feels in pocket again and goes into tent as if searching for something.*)

The Older Man looks at the photo with haggard eyes for a moment, then whispers in a half sob "My wife!" *Then staring into vacancy he speaks to himself, unconsciously aloud:* "She has not changed."

JACK. (*who has come back from the tent with a soiled envelope in his hand in time to hear the last sentence*) (*astonished*) "Changed? Who? Do you know her?"

THE OLDER MAN. (*quickly mastering his emotion and lying bravely*) "No. Of course not. But she reminds me of a girl I knew here in the States a long time ago. But the girl I speak of must be an old woman by this time. I forget my grey hairs."

JACK. "Yvette is only twenty-five. Her parents were poor French people. In a fit of mistaken zeal for her welfare they forced her to marry this man when she was too young to know her own mind. They thought they were making an excellent match. Immediately after the marriage he dragged her off to San Sebastien where he was half owner of a small mine. It seems the devil broke out in him before they were hardly settled there. (*after a pause*) "I'd like to be fair to him. Maybe he realized that she could never love him and was trying to drown the memory of the mistake he had made. He certainly loved her - in his fashion."

THE OLDER MAN. (*in a pathetic whisper*) "Yes. He must have loved her - in his fashion."

JACK. (*looking at the letter in his hand which he had forgotten*) "Ah, I forgot. I have proof positive of her innocence and noble-mindedness. Here is a letter which she wrote and sent to me the morning I was leaving. It's only a few words. Read it Mr. Doubting Thomas. (*hands letter to the Older Man.*)

THE OLDER MAN. (*his hands tremble*) (*aside*) "Her writing" (*reading aloud*) " 'I must keep my oath. He needs me and I must stay. To be true to myself I must be true to him (*aside* "My God I was wrong after all"*) Sometime I may send for you. Good-bye' signed Yvette" (*he folds the letter up slowly, puts it back in the envelope and hands it to Jack. Suddenly he turns to him with quick suspicion*) "What does she mean by that last sentence?"

JACK. "When I left I gave her my address in the States and she promised to let me know if she changed her mind or if conditions changed."

THE OLDER MAN. (*with grim irony*) "You mean if the drunken husband died."

JACK. (*his face growing hard*) "Yes. That's what I mean."

THE OLDER MAN. "Well how do you know he hasn't? Have you ever heard from her since?"

JACK. "Only the one time when she sent the picture I showed you. I received the letter from her in Cape Town a year ago. It had been forwarded from the States. She said her husband had disappeared soon after I left. No one knew where he had gone but the rumor was that he had set out on my trail for vengeance, refusing to believe in her innocence" (*grimly patting his gun*) "I'm sorry he didn't find me."

THE OLDER MAN. (*he has by this time regained control of himself and speaks quite calmly*) "Where is she now?"

JACK. "Living with her parents in New York. She wrote to say that she would wait a year longer. If he did not return to her by then she would become legally free of him and would send for me. The year is up today but (*hopelessly*) I have received no word" (*walks back and looks into the darkness as if hoping to see someone coming.*)

The Older Man suddenly remembers the telegram he has. He takes it from his pocket as if to give it to Jack; then hesitates and says in agony "My God I cannot!" *as he realizes the full significance of what the telegram says. Mastered by a contrary impulse he goes to burn it in the camp fire but again hesitates. Finally as Jack returns slowly to the camp fire he turns quickly and hands the telegram to him.*

THE OLDER MAN. "Cheer up! Here's a surprise for you. Read this. Old Pete brought it from Lawson before you returned and I forgot all about it. I opened it by mistake thinking it might have something to do with the mine. (*he turns quickly away as if unable to bear the sight of Jack's elation.*)

Jack feverishly opens the yellow envelope. His face lights up and he gives an exclamation of joy and rushes to the Older Man.

JACK. "It's too good to be true. Tell me I am not dreaming."

THE OLDER MAN. (*he looks at Jack steadily for a moment, then tries hard to smile and mutters*) "Congratulations" (*he is suffering horribly.*)

JACK. (*misunderstanding the cause of his emotion*) Never mind Old Pal I won't be gone long and when I come back I'll bring her with me."

THE OLDER MAN. (*hastily*) "No. I'll manage all right. Better stay East for a while. We'll need someone there when the work really starts."

JACK. "When can I get a train?"

THE OLDER MAN. "If you ride hard and start right away you can get to Lawson in time for the Limited at three in the morning."

JACK. (*rushing off with saddle under arm*) "My horse is hobbled at the mouth of the canyon."

THE OLDER MAN. (*stands in front of tent*) "So I have found him after all these years and I cannot even hate him. What tricks Fate plays with us. When he told me his name that first day I noticed that it was the same as the man's I was looking for. But he seemed such a boy to me and my heart went out to him so strongly that I never for an instant harbored the idea that he could be the John Sloan I was after. Of course he never knew my right name. I wonder what he would say if he knew. I've half a mind to tell him. But no, what's the use? Why should I mar his happiness? In this affair I alone am to blame and I must pay. As I listened to his story this evening until no doubt remained that he was the John Sloan I had sworn to kill, my hand reached for my gun and all the old hate flared up in my heart. And then I remembered his face as he looked that day in the Transvaal when he bent over me after saving my life at the risk of his own. I could almost hear his words as he spoke that day when death was so near "All right, old pal, you're all right" Then my hand left my gun and the old hatred died out forever. I could not do it. (*he pauses and a bitter smile comes over his face as at some new thought*) "O what a fool I have been. She was true to me in spite of what I was. God bless him for telling me so. God grant they may both be happy - the only two beings I have ever loved. And I - must keep wandering on. I cannot be the ghost at their feast."

JACK. (*entering hurriedly, putting on spurs, hat, etc.*) "Good-bye Old Pal. I'm sorry to leave you this way but I have waited so long for this. You understand don't you?"

THE OLDER MAN. (*slowly*) "Yes" (*grasping his hand and looking deep into his eyes*) "Good-bye and God bless you both."

JACK. (*feelingly*) "Good-bye" (*exits.*)

The Older Man sits down by the camp fire and buries face in his hands. Finally he rouses himself with an effort, stirs the camp fire and smiling with a whimsical sadness softly quotes: "Greater love hath no man than this that he giveth his wife for his friend."

THE CURTAIN FALLS